Forgotten Delights: The Producers

Volume One in the Forgotten Delights series

To purchase 340 color photos
of the sculptures
in this volume on a CD,
visit

www.ForgottenDelights.com

Forthcoming volumes in the Forgotten Delights series include

Defenders

Politicians and Media Moguls

Artists

Allegorical and Mythological Figures

Children and Animals

For locations and fascinating facts about other outdoor sculpture in Manhattan, visit

www.ForgottenDelights.com

Forgotten Delights: The Producers

A Selection of Manhattan's Outdoor Sculpture

by Dianne L. Durante

New York
2003

ISBN 0-9745899-1-8

Additional copies of this book and a
CD with color photos may be ordered at
www.ForgottenDelights.com

Table of Contents

Illustrations

Introduction

The Series Forgotten Delights

Baggy overcoat, mutton-chop whiskers, puzzling object in one hand (could that be an artist's palette?): rushing by, I wonder what this old fuddy-duddy did to deserve an eight-foot-high bronze statue. I can't figure it out from a quick glance, so I keep moving.

The next time I pass by, I notice a Parks Department plaque describing John Ericsson and the *Monitor*. "Esteemed Swedish-American engineer and inventor..." Sounds like an encyclopedia entry. Yawn. Next time I'll keep walking again.

Months later, a crumbling Civil-War-era volume exhumed from the depths of New York Public Library provides details that finally grab my attention. Ericsson, a highly competent naval engineer, was often candid far beyond the point of tact. When Navy bureaucrats rejected his proposed ironclad for completely invalid reasons, he lectured them on its seaworthiness. Then:

> His blood being well warmed by this time, he ended by declaring to the board with great earnestness: "Gentlemen, after what I have said, I consider it to be your duty to the country to give me an order to build the vessel before I leave this room."

Contract in hand, Ericsson returned to New York to supervise the building of the *Monitor*, a radically innovative type of naval vessel, at three different yards in New York, in a hundred days flat.

That's a man worth stopping to look at. Not only did he share my attitude toward obstructive bureaucrats and wasted time, but he was brilliant enough to design a new type of vessel and efficient enough to supervise its construction in record time. These days when I walk by Ericsson's statue, I give him a smile of admiration and comradeship.

Since I "met" *Ericsson*, I've researched many other outdoor sculptures. Now when I'm in Manhattan, I find myself surrounded by fascinating and delightful figures. They make me stop, look and think when I would have sworn my brain was too tired to function. They cheer me up when I'm tired or exasperated. The achievements and the virtues of the people these statues represent help supply the emotional fuel, the psychological energy, that keeps me going.

Forgotten Delights is a series of guidebooks to the sculptures of men, women, children and animals scattered throughout Manhattan, whom most people pass unseeingly and unthinkingly. Each volume in the series will cover a different group:

- Producers (explorers, inventors, engineers, businessmen)
- Defenders (soldiers, policemen, firemen)
- Politicians and Media Moguls (statesmen, politicians, lawyers, publishers, editors, journalists)
- Artists
- Allegorical and Mythological Figures
- Children; Animals

Forgotten Delights: The Producers

"Productive work," wrote Ayn Rand, "is the road of man's unlimited achievement and calls upon the highest attributes of his character: his creative ability, his ambitiousness, his self-assertiveness, his refusal to bear uncontested disasters, his dedication to the goal of reshaping the earth in the image of his values." (For more of this passage, see Essay Number 18 on Johnson's *Taxi,* 1983.)

Forgotten Delights: The Producers is a celebration of explorers, inventors, engineers, businessmen and workers whose thoughts and efforts reshaped New York, the United States and the world, making their lives and ours immeasurably better. Manhattan's outdoor sculptures don't include giants such as Edison, Bell, Carnegie or Ford. Yet the men who are represented are inspiring, both for their achievements and for reminding us that human progress can and should be not a rare occurrence but the norm.

The lives of most of the men discussed in *The Producers* have been chronicled in full-length, scholarly biographies. (See the references at the end of each essay.) Rather than summarizing such accounts, each essay in this book focuses on one of the subject's major achievements and its significance.

The essays are arranged by the dates of these major achievements, rather than by the dates at which the sculptures were cast or carved. Thus arranged, a look at nineteen pieces of sculpture gives a panoramic view of the growth of New York and America across the centuries.

Each of the nineteen essays includes:

- Title
- Artist
- Date of dedication
- Location, with notes on the best conditions for viewing
- "About the Statue": the sculpture as an artwork
- "About the Subject": a major achievement of the person represented, and its significance
- A sidebar with a lengthy quotation by, or related to, the subject of the sculpture
- Bibliography and recommendations for further reading
- Provenance: who paid for the sculpture and who owns it

At the end of the volume are a chronological list of sculptures by date of dedication, a brief annotated bibliography of sources on sculpture and New York, a subject index and (at the very end, for ease of reference) a list of the sculptures arranged for a walking tour.

A note on visiting the sculptures

Because each of these sculptures is a three-dimensional object, one photograph—even several—cannot reveal all its details. To get the full impact, you must visit the sculpture.

The suggested walking tour at the end of the volume can be done in one long day, or broken down into several shorter trips. Take binoculars or a camera with a good telephoto lens, particularly for the *Columbus Monument* at Columbus Circle and the reliefs on the *Ericsson* at Battery Park.

Many sculptures are best observed at certain times of the day or year. On a very sunny day, for example, reflections make it difficult to see details on polished bronze. If a sculpture faces east, its front will fall into impenetrable shadow in the afternoon. If it's set among trees, as many sculptures in Central Park are, the flickering shadows of the leaves often obscure details. I have noted such considerations for each sculpture. My own favorite viewing time is on an autumn day after the leaves have fallen, when the sky is slightly overcast. Bundle up.

You would think an inanimate object weighing several tons would remain in one place. Not true: sculptures are moved, sometimes for cleaning, sometimes because the owner decides they could be displayed to better advantage elsewhere. The locations furnished here are valid as of Spring 2003. If you cannot find a City-owned sculpture in the location given, ask a Parks Department employee for information or try the Parks Department's website (http://www.nycgovparks.org/index.php). If the sculpture is privately owned, the nearest doorman often knows where the work has gone.

Photographs

All but two of the photographs in *Forgotten Delights: The Producers* are my own. (The exceptions are *Double Check* and Saint Gaudens' *Puritan,* shown with *The Pilgrim.*) Since this edition of the book is self-published and color photographs of acceptable quality are extremely expensive to reproduce, I have included only black-and-white photos with the printed text. Over three hundred color photographs, most not shown in the printed text, are available on CD-ROM. To order, visit www.ForgottenDelights.com.

Copyright issues

To the best of my understanding at the present moment (July 10, 2003, 7:14 a.m. EST), sculptures created before 1923 are in the public domain, i.e., are no longer copyright-protected. For sculptures produced after 1923, the copyright is held by the artist rather than the owner of the work, barring a signed agreement to the contrary. When reproducing the image of such a sculpture in a book, on a CD or on the web, the permission of the artist or the artist's estate is required, even if one uses one's own photograph of the sculpture.

Accordingly, I have made sincere efforts to contact the artists of the few works in *Forgotten Delights: The Producers* that were created after 1923, in order to request permission to reproduce their work. My only complete failure was Luis Sanguino, sculptor of *The Immigrants.* If you know how to contact him or his agents, I would be greatly obliged if you would contact me at comments@ForgottenDelights.com.

To complicate matters, a photographer usually holds the copyright to his photograph of a sculpture. Hence even for works dating to 1923 or earlier, the photographs in this book and the accompanying CD (which were all taken within the last few decades) should not be reproduced without the permission of the photographer who is cited as the copyright holder next to the photograph.

Acknowledgements

The research for this book could not have been completed, or even begun, without the magnificent resources of the New York Public Library and the New-York Historical Society Library. The writing could not have been completed without the blissful silence of the New York Society Library. Thanks also to the staffs of the New York City Department of Parks and Recreation, the Art Commission of the City of New York, and the National Sculpture Society for helping me track down obscure pieces, elusive sculptors and photographs of sculptures as they no longer are.

In a series of essays that ranges from Columbus to the Pilgrims to Bessemer steel, it would be delightful but surprising if no factual errors slipped in. If you notice an error, please let me know (comments@ForgottenDelights.com) so I can correct it in the next printing or edition. If possible, please include a bibliographical reference for the correct information.

I am grateful to Bruce Rickard, Lynn Feliziani and Robert Begley, who read and commented on parts of this book before publication.

Finally, thanks to my husband Sal and daughter Allegra, who have listened to the stories and hiked to the sculptures for the past year. My debt to both of you is monumental.

Essay Number 1

1492

The Columbus Monument

Why say: "Sail on! sail on! and on!"
—Miller

Artist: Gaetano Russo

Dedicated: 1892

Medium and size: Overall 77 feet tall. Carrera marble statue of Columbus (13 feet tall). Marble figure of a Genius on the south side (9 feet). Bronze eagle on the north side (6 feet). Bronze reliefs on the south and north sides, each 2 feet by 6 feet. Fountains around base designed by Douglas Leigh. Decorative fence presented to the City in 1960 by the Delacorte Foundation.

Location: Columbus Circle, intersection of Eighth Avenue, Central Park South and 59th Street. The entrances to the island on which the *Monument* sits are at the southwest and northwest sides of the Circle, by the new AOL Time Warner Center. Columbus faces south, and would be easily visible at any time of day if he were not so high: take binoculars.

About the statue

Wait: before we look at the *Columbus Monument*, let me just change a detail here and there. In place of that weird winged figure in front, I'll put someone recognizable: Isabella, Queen of Spain. In place of the two large bronze reliefs, I'll deftly model four smaller ones: Columbus presenting his plans to Spanish authorities; Columbus raising a cross where he made landfall on his first voyage; Columbus received by the king and queen after his return; Columbus in chains following his disastrous stint as colonial administrator. At the corners, I'll add statuettes of men who helped make the first voyage possible: King Ferdinand, Columbus's brother, a monk from La Rábida, a member of the Pinzón family. On the sides, I'll eradicate that inscription praising Columbus' courage and determination in favor of a list the names of the crew from his first voyage. The bronze eagle might scare passing children—off it goes in favor of a cross, large and flamboyantly gothic. And at the top... White's so boring. I'll dress Columbus in the elaborate court robes he wore as Admiral of the Ocean Sea, paint them vivid colors, and give him a Spanish flag to hold.

What have I done by changing "a detail here and there"? I've emphasized that Columbus had flaws as well as virtues (great navigator, lousy colonial administrator), and that he couldn't have succeeded without the help of his family, his patrons, his crew, and his God.

My alterations probably wouldn't have occurred to you. Indeed, a good work of art ought to be so much of a piece, so well integrated, its message so clear and obvious, that you never stop to think it might have been otherwise. Yet when a sculptor is at work he is constantly making choices, and each of those choices—from the position of an eyelid to the set of the chin, from the size of the pedestal to the texture of the face—affects the message we, as viewers, get from a work.

As viewers, we can enjoy sculptures more and understand their messages better if we pay attention to such details. That's why each essay in *Forgotten Delights: The Producers* includes a

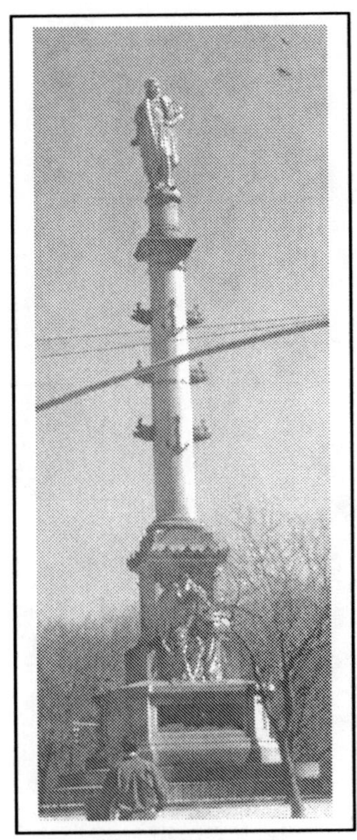

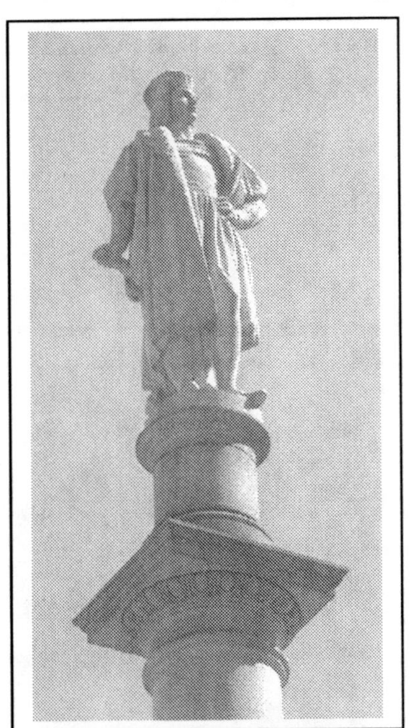

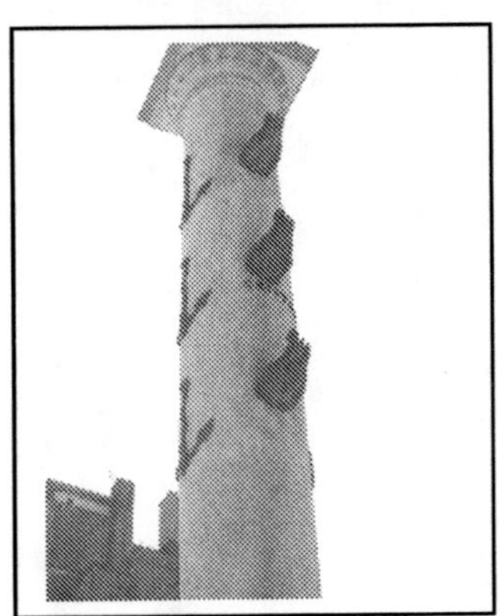

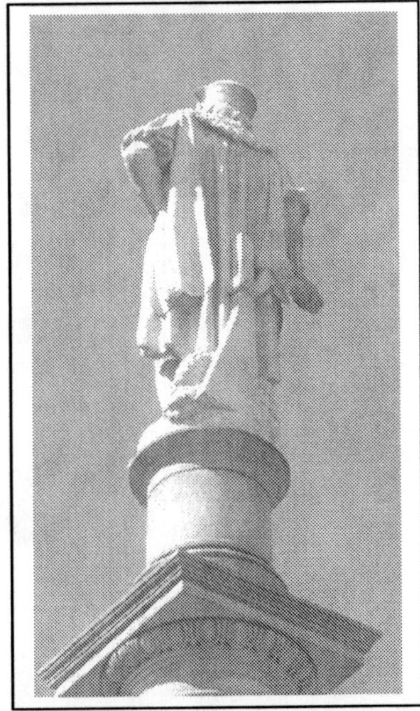

Photos © Dianne L. Durante

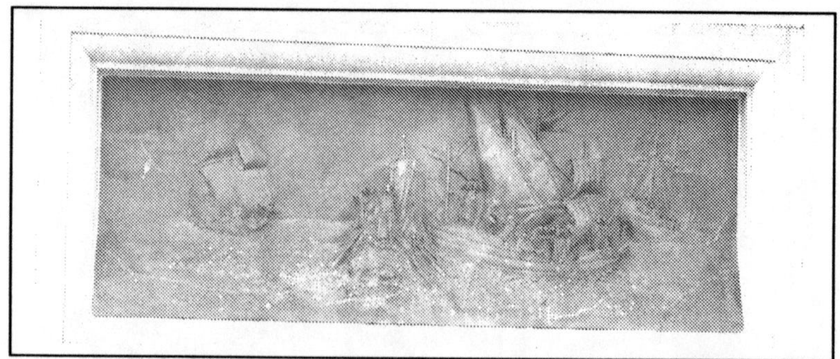

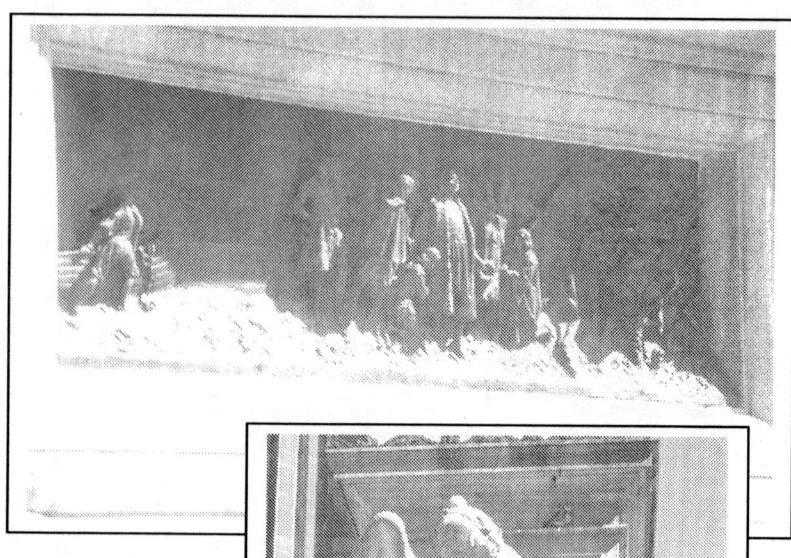

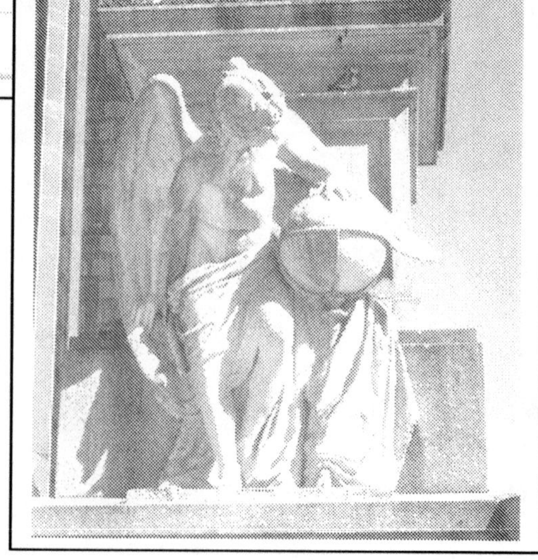

Photos © Dianne L. Durante

section on the statue itself, as well as a section on the person or persons represented.

Now let's look at the *Columbus Monument* as it stands, and see what its message actually is. On the south side (the principal view), the first figure we see is a nine-foot-tall winged boy leaning over a globe. Before his features were eroded, he gazed down at the Americas with a smile of delight. Because he is the first figure the viewer sees closely, he sets the mood for the whole *Monument*. His smile proclaims that the discovery of the Americas was a marvelous accomplishment.

The boy has been called the "Genius of Columbus" and the "Genius of Geography." ("Genius" in this case is a type of guardian deity, not an individual of high intellect.) I prefer to think of the figure as the "Genius of Discovery," a reminder that Columbus' voyage was the impetus for hundreds of later voyages of exploration.

Aside from the Genius, the most striking street-level features of the *Columbus Monument* are two six-foot-wide bronze reliefs. On the north side, below a fierce bronze eagle gripping the shields of Genoa (Columbus' birthplace) and the United States, the relief shows Columbus' fleet anchored in the Caribbean. As his men crowd along the rails, a longboat ferries Columbus to shore.

Columbus is said to have knelt and wept for joy when he landed, but in the relief on the south side (below the Genius) he stands triumphantly, shoulders back, chin raised, gazing upward. The only kneeling figure is a youth who kisses Columbus' hand, gratefully saluting the man who brought the ships to safe harbor. Another companion respectfully touches Columbus' sleeve, as others raise the flag and haul a longboat ashore. One man anxiously draws Columbus' attention to the Indians half-hidden in the trees at the right. In the midst of this crowd, Columbus is unquestionably the dominant figure, whose achievement and authority everyone acknowledges.

Now step back and look above the Genius and the reliefs. The pillar that supports Columbus' statue displays five anchors, recalling a section of the coat of arms awarded to Columbus after his first voyage. Balancing the anchors are three pairs of rostra, the beak-like prows of ancient ships, designed to ram enemy vessels. The Roman emperor Augustus mounted the prows of his enemies' ships on a column after the decisive Battle of Actium in 31 B.C., and ever since they have symbolized victory at sea. Here they represent Columbus's triumph in finding land, as well as the three ships he took on his first voyage.

Atop the column, the colossal figure of Columbus stands proudly upright, chin level, gazing into the distance to his left. The hubbub of traffic and crowds in Columbus Circle can't distract him, since he's sixty feet above them. The left arm, set akimbo, suggests he has energy to spare: imagine the difference if his hands dangled limply, or were folded placidly in front of him. His right hand reaches behind him to the tiller, so that he can steer without turning his eyes from the distant horizon.

All the elements of the *Columbus Monument* unite to present Columbus as the energetic, courageous and focused explorer who deserves full credit for the discovery of the New World. The monument's inscription, in Italian and English, states that explicitly: "To Christopher Columbus, the Italians resident in America. Scoffed at before, during the voyage menaced, after it chained, as generous as oppressed, to the world he gave a world."

"Columbus"

Behind him lay the gray Azores,
Behind the Gates of Hercules;
Before him not the ghost of shores,
Before him only shoreless seas.
The good mate said: "Now must we pray,
For lo! the very stars are gone.
Brave Adm'r'l, speak; what shall I say?"
"Why say: 'Sail on! sail on! and on!'"

"My men grow mutinous day by day;
My men grow ghastly wan and weak."
The stout mate thought of home; a spray
Of salt wave washed his swarthy cheek.

"What shall I say, brave Adm'r'l, say
If we sight naught but seas at dawn?"
"Why, you shall say, at break of day:
'Sail on! sail on! sail on! and on!'"

They sailed and sailed, as winds might blow,
Until at last the blanched mate said:
"Why, now not even God would know
Should I and all my men fall dead.
These very winds forget their way,
For God from these dread seas is gone.
Now speak, brave Adm'r'l; speak and say" —
He said: "Sail on! sail on! and on!"

They sailed. They sailed. Then spake the mate:
"This mad sea shows his teeth to-night;
He curls his lips, he lies in wait,
With lifted teeth, as if to bite:
Brave Adm'r'l, say but one good word;
What shall we do when hope is gone?"
The words leapt like a leaping sword:
"Sail on! sail on! sail on! and on!"

Then, pale and worn, he kept his deck,
And peered through darkness. Ah, that night
Of all dark nights! And then a speck—
A light! a light! a light! a light!
It grew, a starlit flag unfurled!
It grew to be Time's burst of dawn.
He gained a world; he gave that world
Its grandest lesson: "On! sail on!"

—Cincinnatus Hiner Miller
(known as Joaquin Miller), d. 1913

About the subject

Your ship is the length of a basketball court. For weeks you've seen nothing beyond it but saltwater and seaweed. To calculate your direction, you have a magnetized needle stuck on a piece of cardboard. Of course, if this primitive compass isn't properly aligned with the keel, or if a nearby mass of metal (a cannon, say) interferes with it, you'll veer far off course. To tell time you have an hourglass—but when your ship pitches and rolls the sand flows erratically, and there's always the chance that a lazy ship's boy will tuck the hourglass inside his shirt to make his time on duty "run out" more quickly. To gauge your speed, you make an educated guess about how fast you're moving over open sea, without landmarks.

Combine these calculations of direction, time and speed and you have "dead reckoning," the usual method of navigation in Columbus' time. In Miller's poem (see sidebar), the first mate pleads,

> "What shall I say, brave Adm'r'l, say
> If we sight naught but seas at dawn?"

With such technology, how many of us would have the courage to reply:

> "Why, you shall say, at break of day:
> 'Sail on! sail on! sail on! and on!'"

Columbus (ca. 1451-1506) was not the first man to believe the world was round. The Greeks knew it. Many Renaissance scholars knew it. Sailors knew it, from watching ships disappear hull-first over the horizon.

Nor was Columbus the first to dream of reaching Asia by sea. For much of the fifteenth century, the Portuguese had been inching their way down the west coast of Africa. By 1487, when Columbus was still seeking funding for his voyage, Bartolomeo Diaz had rounded the Cape of Good Hope, and in 1498 Vasco da Gama reached India.

Columbus was not even the first European to reach America. The Vikings had landed there centuries earlier, and Europeans had been frequenting Nova Scotia's rich fishing grounds for years.

Columbus's unique and glorious achievement is that he conceived the idea of sailing west in order to reach the Far East, that he had the courage and perseverance to organize and carry out such a voyage, and that he discovered the Americas at the end of it. On his four voyages he established the transatlantic routes that continued in use until steam replaced sail in the nineteenth century. These efficient, predictable sea routes made permanent settlement in the Americas feasible.

Columbus and his brother appealed unsuccessfully for funds and ships to the sovereigns of Portugal, Spain, England and France. Only Queen Isabella of Spain held out hope: ask me again, she said, when the Moors have been driven out of their last stronghold in Spain. And indeed, she finally agreed to fund the "Enterprise of the Indies" soon after Boabdil, the last Moorish ruler, fled Granada. Following an acrimonious debate with Columbus over the titles and property that would be awarded to him if he succeeded, Ferdinand and Isabella signed Columbus' contract in April 1492, six years after he had first sought their support.

Compared with his struggles with royalty and palace bureaucrats, Columbus' battle with the perils of the sea was perhaps a welcome relief. The 85-foot *Santa Maria*, 69-foot *Pinta* and 55-foot *Niña*, with a total of about ninety men, set out from Palos in August 1492 and dropped south to the Canary Islands. In early September, as they left the Islands, Columbus instructed his captains simply to go "west; nothing to the north, nothing to the south." By early October the fleet had covered 2,400 miles, the total distance that Columbus had calculated lay between Spain and Japan. (The distance is actually three times that.)

Only floating tree limbs and other tokens of nearby land prevented mutiny among a crew that had probably never ventured out of sight of land for more than two weeks. On October 12, 1492, amid great rejoicing, the three ships anchored in the Caribbean, and a landing party went ashore—the moment shown in the southern relief of the *Columbus Monument*.

"To the world he gave a world": the *Columbus Monument* is a paean to the heroic navigator who inspired not only future explorers, but anyone undertaking a long, arduous task whose rewards are uncertain but potentially tremendous.

Bibliography and further reading

For contemporary accounts of the *Columbus Monument*, see *New York Times* articles of 6/13/1892, 10/10/1892 and 10/13/1892, and Nestor Ponce de Leon, *The Columbus Gallery: The 'Discoverer of the New World' As Represented in Portraits, Monuments, Statues, Medals and Paintings: Historical Description* (New York, 1893), pp. 116-7, available at http://columbus.vanderkrogt.net/ponce_de_leon.html. Stokes, *The Iconography of Manhattan Island 1498-1909* (New York, 1967 reprint; referred to henceforth as "Stokes"), 5:2011. See also Margot Gayle and Michele Cohen, *The Art Commission and the Municipal Art Society Guide to Manhattan's Outdoor Sculpture* (henceforth "Gayle & Cohen") pp. 263-4, and Martin Reynolds, *Monuments and Masterpieces: Histories and Views of Public Sculpture in New York City* (henceforth "Reynolds"), pp. 341-3, with an early photo of the *Genius*. Smithsonian Institution Research Information System (henceforth "SIRIS," www.siris.si.edu/, click "Search Art Inventories" under "Smithsonian American Art Museum Research Databases") control #IAS 76003475.

On Columbus' early years and first voyage, see Samuel Eliot Morison, *The Great Explorers: The European Discovery of America* (New York & London, 1978), especially Chapters 12-15. Morison's Pulitzer-Prize-winning *Admiral of the Ocean Sea* (originally published in 1942) is a classic biography of Columbus, still essential. For more recent biographies see the annotated list at the end of Felipe Fernandez-Armesto's "Columbus, Christopher," http://www.anb.org/articles/20/2000200.html; American National Biography Online Feb. 2000.

On Boabdil, the last Moorish ruler of Granada, see the forthcoming Forgotten Delights volume on defenders.

Provenance

Inscription on east side of monument: "To Christopher Columbus, The Italians Resident in America. Scoffed at before, during the voyage, menaced, after it, chained, as generous as oppressed, to the world he gave a world." [Below, to the left:] "Joy and glory never uttered a more thrilling call than that which resounded from the conquered ocean in sight of the first American island Land! Land!" [To the right:] "On the

XII of October MDCCCXCII the fourth centenary of the discovery of America in imperishable remembrance."

On the west side of the monument, the same message appears in Italian: "A Cristoforo Colombo gli Italiani residente in America irriso prima minacciato durante il viaggio incatenato dopo sapendo esser generoso quanto oppresso donava un mondo al mondo." [Below left:] "La gioia e la gloria non ebbero mai piu solenne guido di quello che risuono in vista della prima isola americana Terra! Terra!" [Below right:] "Nel 12 ottobre 1892 quarto centenario della scoperta d'America a imperitura memoria."

Gift of Italian-Americans through a public subscription organized by Carlo Barsotti, editor of *Il Progresso Italo-Americano*, the leading Italian-American newspaper in early twentieth-century New York. Collection of the City of New York.

Essay Number 2

1506

Christopher Columbus

It is the object of the following work, to relate the deeds and fortunes of the mariner who ... by his hardy genius, his inflexible constancy, and his heroic courage, brought the ends of the earth into communication with each other.

–Irving

Artist: Jeronimo Suñol

Dedicated: 1894

Medium and size: Bronze (8 feet), pedestal (7 feet) by Napoleon Le Brun.

Location: Central Park, south end of the Mall, near the Literary Walk. (If the grid of the city streets ran through the Park, Columbus would be at about Sixth Avenue and 66th Street.) The sculpture faces east, and is best seen in the morning when the sun is on its face. Since it's among many trees, it's easier to see after the leaves have fallen.

About the statue

What a shocking change from the *Columbus Monument*: here Columbus has a wrinkled brow, bags under his eyes, deep lines at the corners of his mouth, a slight double chin and a receding hairline. Hatless and humble, he gazes heavenward. This appears to be Columbus in his final years (he died in 1506), after a disastrous stint as a colonial administrator and exhausting legal battles to collect the rewards he considered due from his 1492 royal contract. Around his neck on a heavy chain is a portrait of a woman—most likely Queen Isabella, his most influential patron, who died while Columbus's case was plodding through the courts.

Washington Irving on Columbus

Certain it is that at the beginning of the fifteenth century, when the most intelligent minds were seeking in every direction for the scattered lights of geographical knowledge, a profound ignorance prevailed among the learned as to the western regions of the Atlantic; its vast waters were regarded with awe and wonder, seeming to bound the world as with a chaos, into which conjecture could not penetrate, and enterprise feared to adventure. ... It is the object of the following work, to relate the deeds and fortunes of the mariner who first had the judgment to divine, and the intrepidity to brave the mysteries of this perilous deep; and who, by his hardy genius, his inflexible constancy, and his heroic courage, brought the ends of the earth into communication with each other. The narrative of his troubled life is the link which connects the history of the old world with that of the new.

—Washington Irving, *The Life and Voyages of Christopher Columbus*, 1828

Columbus' left hand gestures rather ineffectually. Is he pointing to something? Making a request? We'll come back to this in Essay Number 9, on Vanderbilt (1857), but for now, we can say

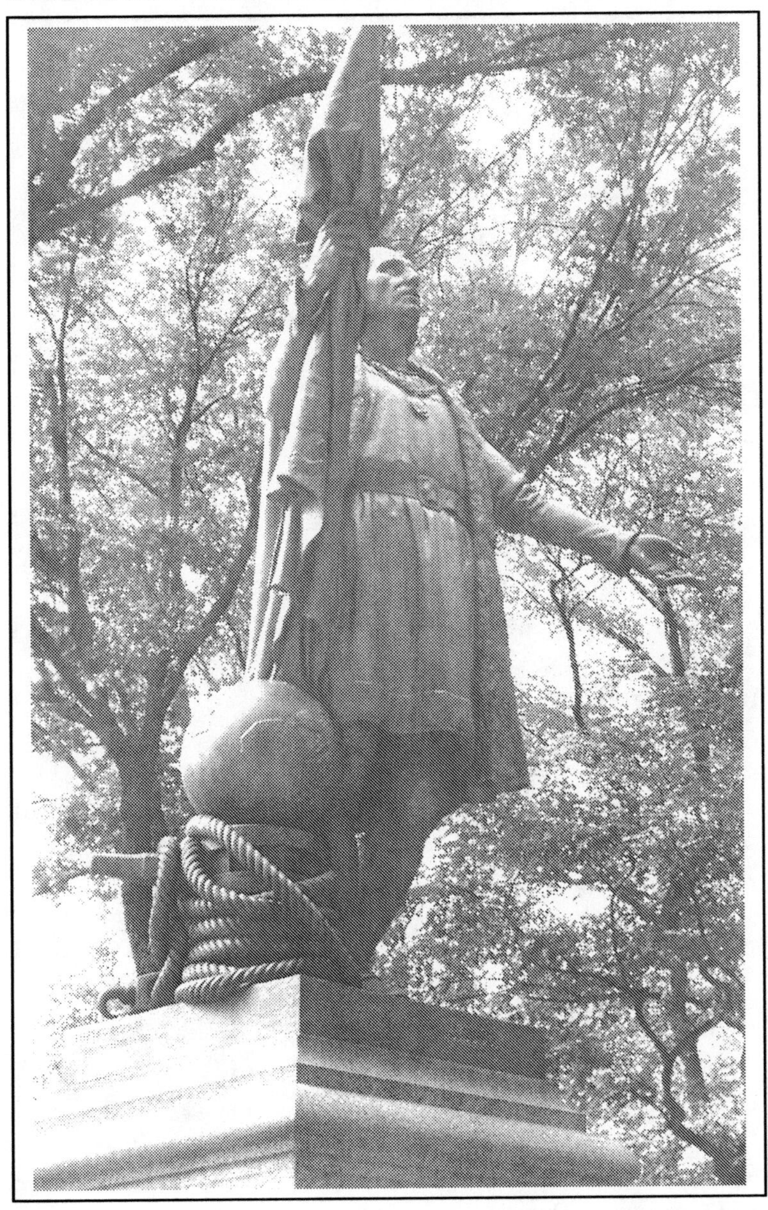

Photo © Dianne L. Durante

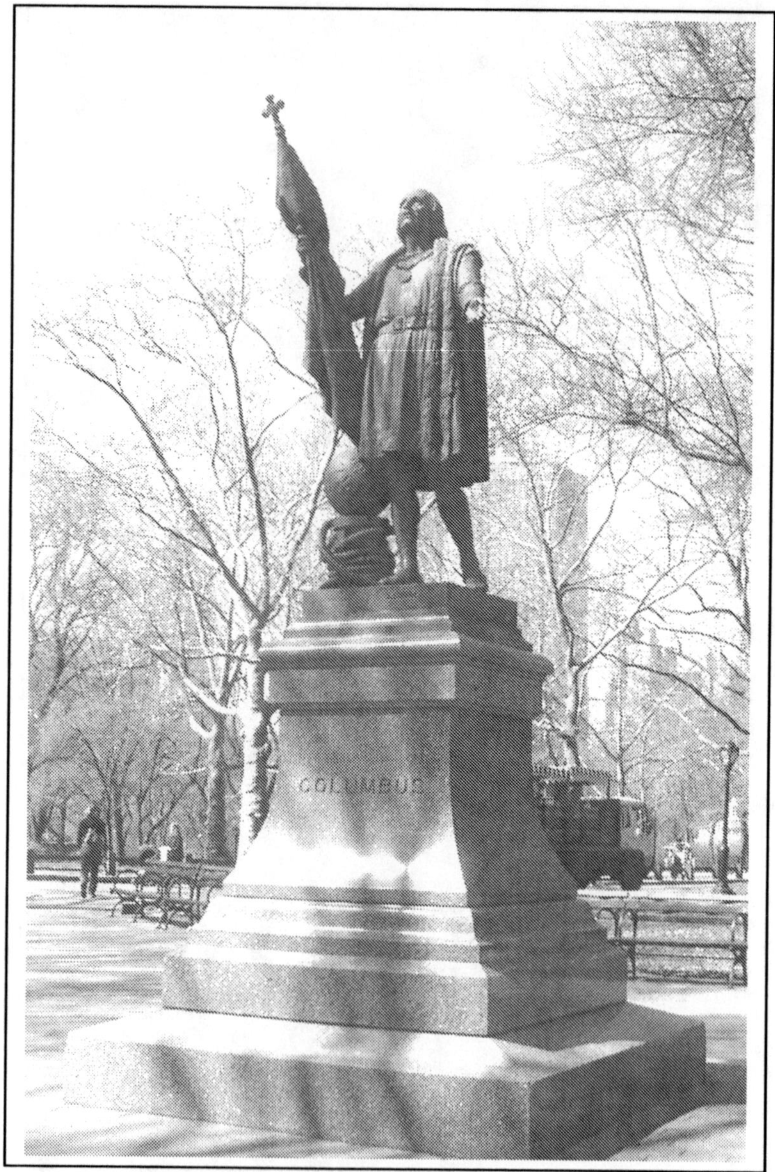

Photo © Dianne L. Durante

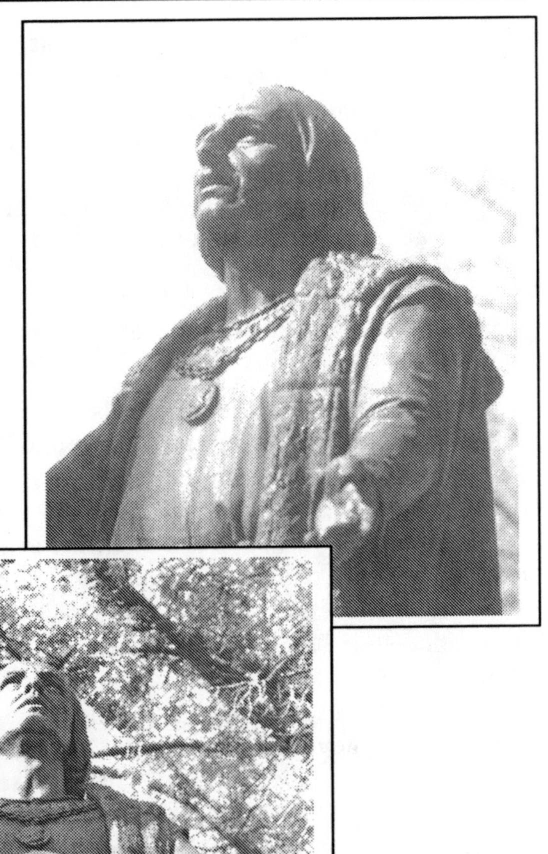

Photos ©
Dianne L. Durante

that the gesture is certainly much less energetic and decisive than the arm-akimbo pose of the *Columbus Monument*.

Behind *Columbus* is a capstan, used on ships to wind in rope. The globe resting on it is the only reference in this sculpture to Columbus' heroic journey beyond the known ends of the earth.

Columbus's right hand grasps a flag bearing the arms of Spain, with its flagpole surmounted by a cross—reminders that Columbus made his voyage with royal authority, and for religious as well as commercial reasons. In his report on the first voyage he asserted,

> For this all Christendom ought to feel joyful and make celebrations and give solemn thanks to the Holy Trinity with many solemn prayers for the great exaltation which it will have, in the turning of so many peoples to our holy faith, and afterwards for material benefits, since not only Spain but all Christians will hence have refreshment and profit. (Quoted in Morison.)

Why can we see all these details? Because the Central Park statue's pedestal is a mere seven feet high. This *Columbus* is literally more down-to-earth than the *Columbus Monument*, where the explorer is poised sixty feet above the ground.

The Central Park statue is a modified version of a marble *Columbus* by Suñol dedicated in Madrid's Plaza de Colón in 1886. That *Columbus* stands on a tall octagonal pillar with an elaborate late-gothic-style base. The base encloses reliefs of the Madonna, Queen Isabella, Columbus conferring with Father Deza, and the *Santa Maria*, plus four life-size heralds, the arms of Spain and a list of crew members. It's similar, in fact, to my *Columbus Monument* with "a detail or two" changed (see Essay Number 1), and its message is the same: that Columbus's achievements were committee efforts, with credit going to God, Spanish monarchs and crew as well as Columbus. The Central Park *Columbus*, bereft of his supporting cast, looks fatigued and hopeless.

About the subject

The attitude of most late-nineteenth-century Americans toward their country was reflected in a single sentence recited by the nation's schoolchildren: "I pledge allegiance to my Flag and the Republic for which it stands: one Nation, indivisible, with Liberty and Justice for all." The Pledge of Allegiance was introduced across the nation on Columbus Day, 1892, the four hundredth anniversary of Columbus's discovery of America. That's appropriate because Americans' attitudes toward Columbus, toward the United States and toward Western civilization have always been closely linked. Washington Irving (see sidebar) was one of the first to make this connection. By 1892 Columbus was regarded as an American national hero, although he never set foot on what became United States soil.

The four-hundredth anniversary of Columbus' first voyage saw the erection of monuments to the explorer throughout the United States, as well as the magnificent, six-month-long Columbian Exposition in Chicago that drew 20 million visitors. Celebrating America's centuries of progress in the intellectual, technological and cultural arenas, the "White City's" 686-acre site was filled with the works of such eminent architects as Richard Morris Hunt, McKim, Mead and White, and Louis H. Sullivan, and was lavishly embellished with sculptures by Frederick MacMonnies, Daniel Chester French, Philip Martiny and others, under the direction of Augustus Saint Gaudens. The Palace of Fine Art's 1,200 paintings and sculptures were the largest display of American works ever assembled, influencing American art until World War I. Other Columbian Exposition displays equated progress with material improvement, glorifying both.

A century later the National Council of Churches, in a widely publicized tirade, shrieked that Columbus' arrival in the Americas brought "an invasion and colonization with legalized occupation, genocide, economic exploitation and a deep level of institutional racism and moral decadence." Few came to Columbus' defense. The five-hundredth anniversary of his first voyage passed in 1992 with only minor tributes.

Yet the debate over whether Columbus' voyage to the New World deserves praise or condemnation is ultimately a debate over whether Western civilization is better than the life of the pre-Columbian "noble savage"—the exhausting, brutally short life of primitive farmers and hunters in a Stone-Age culture where writing and the wheel were unknown. "Some cultures are better than others," writes Dr. Michael Berliner:

> A free society is better than slavery; reason is better than brute force as a way to deal with other men; productivity is better than stagnation. In fact, Western civilization stands for man at his best. It stands for the values that make human life possible: reason, sci-

ence, self-reliance, individualism, ambition, productive achievement. The values of Western civilization are values for all men; they cut across gender, ethnicity, and geography. We should honor Western civilization not for the ethnocentric reason that some of us happen to have European ancestors but because it is the objectively superior culture.

Bibliography and further reading

The dedication ceremonies for this sculpture were privately printed under the title *Presentation of Suñol's Bronze Statue of Christopher Columbus The Mall, Central Park, New York, Saturday, May 12, 1894* (1894). See also Nestor Ponce de Leon, *The Columbus Gallery: The 'Discoverer of the New World' As Represented in Portraits, Monuments, Statues, Medals and Paintings: Historical Description* (New York, 1893), p. 122, who mentions that the Suñol replica in New York is soon to be dedicated. Suñol's Madrid statue is described on the Columbus Monuments Pages, http://columbus.vanderkrogt.net /es/madrid1.html. Gayle & Cohen p. 204. SIRIS control #IAS 87870160.

On Columbus, see the bibliography for the *Columbus Monument.* On Columbus and the value of Western civilization, see Michael Berliner, "On Columbus Day, Celebrate Western Civilization, Not Multiculturalism" (op-ed for The Ayn Rand Institute, www.aynrand.org /medialink/columbus.html), and Thomas Bowden, *The Enemies of Christopher Columbus* (Paper Tiger, 2003). For an interesting description of America before Columbus, see Charles C. Mann, "1491" (*Atlantic Monthly*, 3/2002; http://www.the atlantic.com/issues /2002 /03/mann.htm).

Provenance

Inscription on front of pedestal: "Columbus." On back: "Presented by the citizens of New York in commemoration of the four hundredth anniversary of the discovery of the New World October 1492."

General James Grant Wilson, who saw Suñol's 1886 marble *Columbus* in the Plaza de Colón in Madrid, led the drive to have a bronze replica (slightly modified by the artist) cast for New York. Under the auspices of the New York Genealogical Society, the Astors, Vanderbilts, Rockefellers and other prominent New Yorkers contributed $100 each toward the price of the statue. Collection of the City of New York.

Essay Number 3

1524

Giovanni da Verrazzano

A very pleasant place, situated amongst certain little steep hills ... –Verrazzano

Artist: Ettore Ximenes

Dedicated: 1909

Medium and size: Overall about 22 feet high. Bronze bust (5 feet), allegorical figure (9 feet). Later granite base. Badly in need of a cleaning as of July 2003.

Location: Battery Park, near the waterfront, just east of Castle Clinton. The sculpture faces south, so it is in the sun most of the day, but the flickering shadows from the leaves above it make it difficult to see.

About the statue

Verrazzano has a swashbuckling, arrogant appeal. Of heroic size (the bust alone is five feet tall), he holds his right arm akimbo while his left hand grasps the cape sweeping down from his armor. His face, turned alertly to one side, displays the features recorded in nearly contemporary portraits of Verrazzano:

Roman nose (the sort that goes from forehead to tip without a dent at eye level), heavy but well-groomed beard and mustache. The lower edge of the cape, which originally curved around the base and linked him more closely to the allegorical figure below, was lopped off when the statue's deteriorated and vandalized pedestal was replaced in 1951.

And what about that allegorical figure, whom Jewell described as a "strong-minded 'symbolic' female staring glumly ahead"? With her long hair and flowing drapery she's an effective foil to the martial *Verrazzano,* but who is she?

Gayle and Cohen call her "Discovery." The 1909 *New York Times* account of the unveiling calls her "Truth." The Italian inscription refers to both Justice and Truth (*giustizia* and *verita*), for this statue is more than a monument: it's a polemic. In 1909 New York City was honoring Henry Hudson, an Englishman in Dutch pay who, in 1609, was the first European to sail up the river that now bears his name. Italian-Americans were offended that the 1909 celebrations ignored Verrazzano, the first European to sail into New York Harbor. Justice and truth required (they argued) that Verrazzano be recognized as the first European to gaze upon the not-yet-called-Hudson River.

The flaming torch in the woman's left hand, long since lost, was a symbol of enlightenment – literally "shedding light" on a subject. (The *Statue of Liberty*, sometimes known as *Liberty Enlightening the World*, uses the same symbolism.) The sword with which the figure pierces the book at her feet (opened to show the dates 1524 and 1909) represents the sharp wits needed to see history clearly.

That said, the identification of the woman as Discovery, Truth or Justice isn't obvious from the statue itself. Allegorical figures can be confusing if the artist doesn't use details that clearly and unequivocally convey the abstract idea he has in mind—a matter I'll discuss in the forthcoming Forgotten Delights volume on allegorical figures.

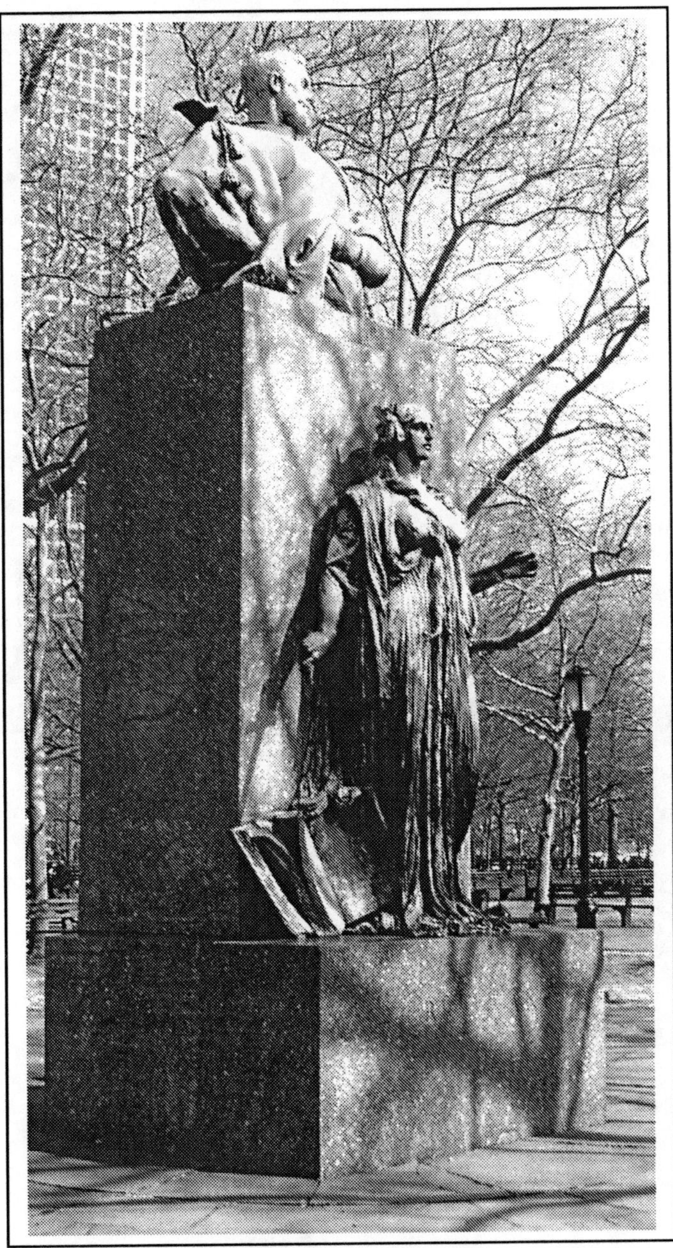

Photo © Dianne L. Durante

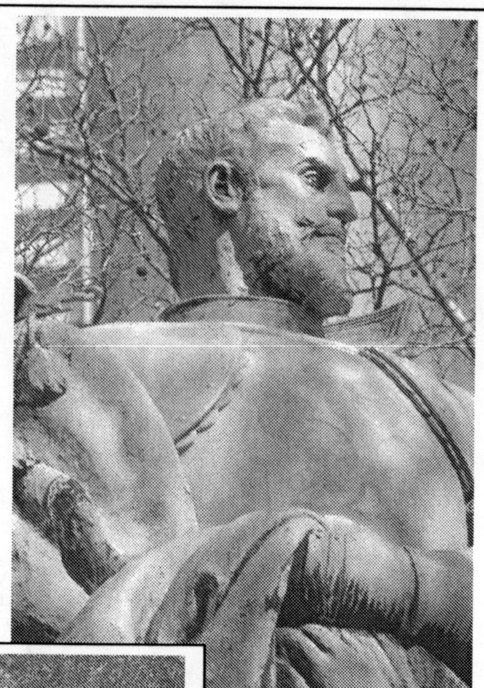

Photos © Dianne L. Durante

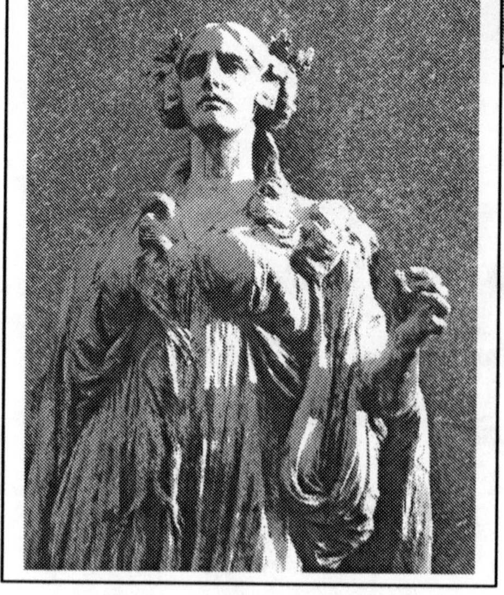

Verrazzano on New York Harbor

We found a very pleasant place, situated amongst certain little steep hills; from amidst the which hills there ran down into the sea a great stream of water, which within the mouth was very deep, and from the sea to the mouth of same, with the tide, which we found to rise 8 foot, any great vessel laden may pass up. ... But because we rode at anchor in a place well fenced from the wind, we would not venture ourselves without knowledge of the place, and we passed up with our boat only into the said river, and saw the country very well peopled. The people are almost like unto the others, and clad with feathers of fowls of divers colors. They came towards us very cheerfully, making great shouts of admiration, showing us where we might come to land most safely with our boat. We entered up the said river into the land about half a league, where it made a most pleasant lake about three leagues in compass; on the which they rowed from the one side to the other, to the number of thirty of their small boats, wherein were many people, which passed from one shore to the other to come and see us. And behold, upon the sudden (as it is wont to fall out in sailing) a contrary flaw of the wind coming from the sea, we were enforced to return to our ship, leaving this land, to our great discontentment for the great commodity and pleasantness thereof, which we suppose is not without some riches, all the hills showing mineral matters in them. —Verrazzano, 1524 (quoted in Morison, p.153)

About the subject

The first European sighting of New York Harbor was made by an explorer seeking financial gain for his backers. Fittingly, New York rose to greatness not as a center of government but as a thriving commercial hub.

Why was an Italian-born navigator working for the King of France sailing these waters? In 1522 the tattered remnant of Magellan's fleet (one of his original five ships, eighteen of his 239 men) reached Lisbon's harbor. The published report of this first voyage around the world inspired an intense rivalry between European monarchs to discover a route to Asia that would bypass the treacherous South-American strait bearing Magellan's name. In the thirty years between Columbus' first voyage and Magellan's circumnavigation, much of the coast of Central and South America had been explored. Further north, the area around Newfoundland was thoroughly familiar to fishermen. In seeking a passage through the American continent, therefore, Verrazzano set out for the Atlantic coast of what is today the United States.

Francis I of France, who had a high regard for Italians (Leonardo da Vinci and Benevenuto Cellini were honored guests at his court), provided Verrazzano with the *Dauphine*. Italian merchants based in France funded the voyage, hoping Verrazzano would find a route to Asia that would reduce the cost of importing silk.

Verrazzano's first landfall was at Cape Fear, on North Carolina's Outer Banks—a chain of islands twenty miles or so from the mainland. Unable to see land beyond the Banks and unable to find a passage through, Verrazzano concluded that he was looking at the Pacific Ocean. Thus the expedition's mapmaker drew it, and thus it remained on many maps for another hundred years.

After sailing down the coast as far as South Carolina in fruitless search of a passage, Verrazzano headed north. Somehow he failed to sight the entrances to the Chesapeake and Delaware Bays. Perhaps he sailed too far from the coast, fearing he might run aground.

But New York Harbor he did not miss, and on April 17, 1524, he described it as "a very pleasant place, situated amongst certain little steep hills." (See sidebar.) Anchoring in the Narrows, he was warmly greeted by Indians and was disappointed when a sudden squall forced him to move on. The area, which he dubbed "Angoulême" after one of the French king's estates, clearly made a better impression on Verrazzano and his crew than southern Maine—labeled on the expedition's map "Terra onde he mala gente" (Land of the Bad People).

Based on his explorations, Verrazzano concluded that the continent whose coast he had been exploring might possibly be attached to Northern Europe in the Arctic regions, but was not connected to any part of Asia. Verrazzano's sponsors were not impressed with this negative conclusion, and the French funded no further expeditions to or settlements on the mid-Atlantic Coast—which is why we don't sing "I'll make a brand new start of it in old Angoulême."

Bibliography and further reading

For the unveiling of the *Verrazzano*, see *New York Times* 10/7/1909. Jewell's article, "Winds of Scorn for Our Statues," is in the *Times* 8/21/1938. Gayle & Cohen p. 7: photo shows the original base. SIRIS control #IAS 76002844.

On Verrazzano, see Norman J. W. Thrower, "Verrazzano, Giovanni da" (http://www.anb.org/articles/20/20-01225.html; American National Biography Online Feb. 2000). See also Samuel Eliot Morison's *The Great Explorers: The European Discovery of America* (New York, 1986), especially Ch. 5. Lawrence C. Wroth's *The Voyages of Giovanni da Verrazzano 1524-1528* (1970) contains a translation and a transcription of Verrazzano's letter to Francis I, an extensive bibliography, and maps. On other early voyages to the site of modern New York, see Burrows and Wallace, *Gotham*, Ch. 1. (Note: The bridge named after Verrazzano is inexplicably spelled with only one "z".)

The *Henry Hudson* statue proposed in 1909 was finally dedicated in the Bronx in 1938. When Robert Moses requested City funds to illuminate it, Deputy Mayor Curran caustically replied, "I took a good look yesterday at the statue of Henry Hudson at Spuyten Duyvil ... It is the ugliest statue in New York, and that is saying a whole lot. The shaft is ugly, the figure is ugly, the whole thing is ugly. A barber pole would be nicer. Now just forget your idea of lighting it up at night. If you could dig a hole at Spuyten Duyvil and let the statue drop into it some night, and then cover it nicely, that would be the best way to handle it." (Quoted by Jewell in the *Times*, 8/21/1938.)

Provenance

The inscription on the back of the base reads, "In April 1524 the Florentine-born navigator Verrazzano led the French caravel La Dauphine to the discovery of the Harbor of New York and named these shores 'Angoulême,' in honor of Francis I, King of France." On the west side: "Anno 1909 America e Italia ricordano Giovanni da Verrazzano fiorentino che primo europeo precorrendo altro piu fortunato dal quale ebbero il nome navigo queste acque le cui terre erano destinate per una delle citta capital del mondo." (Roughly translated: "In 1909, America and Italy remember Giovanni da Verrazzano, Florentine, who was the first European—preceding the fortunate sailor [Hudson] after whom they were named–to navigate these waters, whose shores were destined to become one of the leading cities of the world.") On the east side: "Per la verita secolare per la giustizia della storia questo monumento rivendicatore eresse Il Progresso Italo-Americano Carlo Barsotti editore la colonia italiana concorde il VI ottobre MCMIX." (Roughly translated: "For the sake of historical truth and justice, this monument was erected by *Il Progresso Italo-Americano*, edited by Carlo Barsotti, with the support of the Italians resident in New York, 6 October 1909.")

Gift of Carlo Barsotti, editor of the newspaper *Il Progresso Italo-Americano*, in the name of the Italians of New York. Collection of the City of New York.

Essay Number 4

1620

The Pilgrim

And the heavy night hung dark,
The hills and waters o'er,
When a band of exiles moored their bark
On the wild New England shore...
—Hemans

Artist: John Quincy Adams Ward

Dedicated: 1885

Medium and size: Bronze (9 feet), on a granite pedestal by Richard Morris Hunt (7.5 feet); 4 bronze bas-reliefs, each 10 x 25 inches.

Location: Central Park, north of the 72nd-Street traverse. Walk into the Park at East 72nd Street, stay on the north side of the sidewalk, and you will see the statue up the hill to the right just as the 72nd-Street traverse splits into east- and west-bound lanes. The statue faces west, and is best seen in the afternoon. Because it sits among a fair number of trees, it is easier to see when the leaves have fallen.

About the statue

Although Ward's *Pilgrim* and Saint Gaudens' *Puritan* were both sculpted in the early 1880s and both represent a historical type rather than a specific individual, they convey radically different messages. Ward's is a wilderness settler, a trader and a religious man. Saint Gaudens' is a militant Christian.

How can we tell? Saint Gaudens' *Puritan* has the broad, lined face of a man well advanced in years. Heavily shadowed by a hat and a high collar, the face's only clearly visible feature is an exceedingly grim mouth. The hefty figure strides vigorously toward us, one hand gripping a huge Bible, the other a thick, knobby staff. His sweeping cape makes him almost as broad as he is tall.

Ward's *Pilgrim*, in contrast, stands upright but at ease. His weight is on his back foot: he isn't moving or even poised to move. Armed for earthly battles, he grasps the muzzle of a musket with one hand and wears extra ammunition cartridges slung across his chest. The wide-brimmed hat tops the face of a rather young man who gazes not heavenward, but alertly into the distance.

The subsidiary details of the statues and their original settings are also critical in distinguishing Ward's and Saint Gaudens' interpretations of the early Massachusetts settlers. Saint Gaudens' statue once loomed atop a six-foot pedestal at the far end of a long, narrow park. Once you entered, you were confronted with this seven-foot figure, almost as tall as he is wide, striding directly toward you. "One way or another," the menacing, militant Christian with his Bible and his club seems to say, "I will make you believe as I do." Saint Gaudens' *Puritan* represents a man who came to America for the right to practice a certain religion, and did not tolerate any deviation from it.

In contrast, Ward's *Pilgrim* was set in the rolling hills and open fields of Central Park, many yards back from the sidewalk. We can walk up to examine the statue, or just stroll by. The figure is much less aggressive and its setting is much less confining.

The reliefs on the *Pilgrim's* pedestal reinforce that mood. On the front, a thick book labeled "Holy Bible" is closed over a

RIGHT:
Saint Gaudens, *Puritan* (Springfield, Massachusetts). Courtesy of the Saint Gaudens National Historic Site.

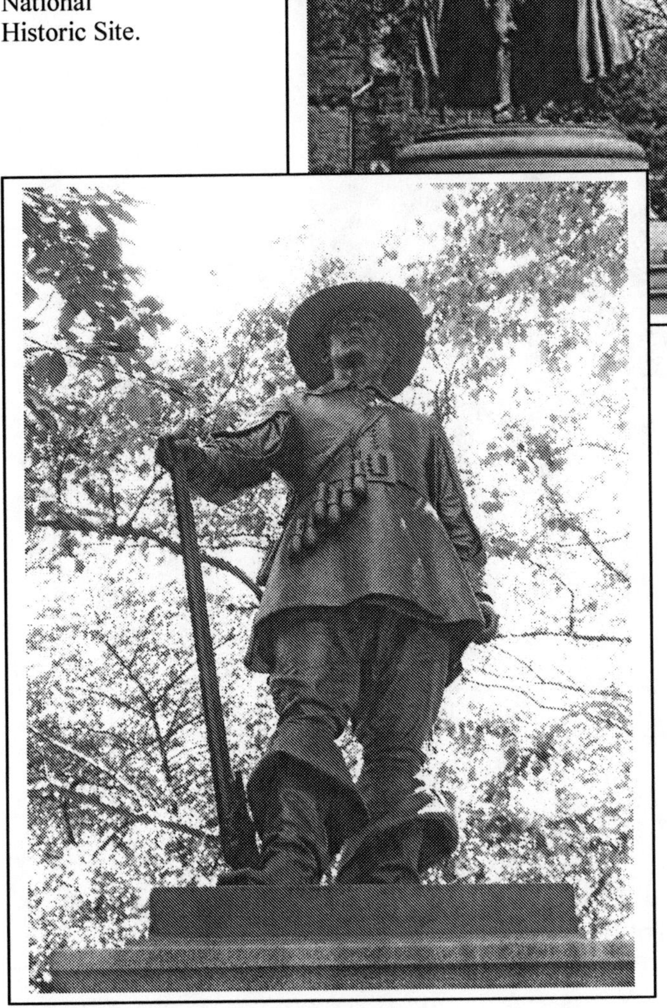

ABOVE: Photo © Dianne L. Durante

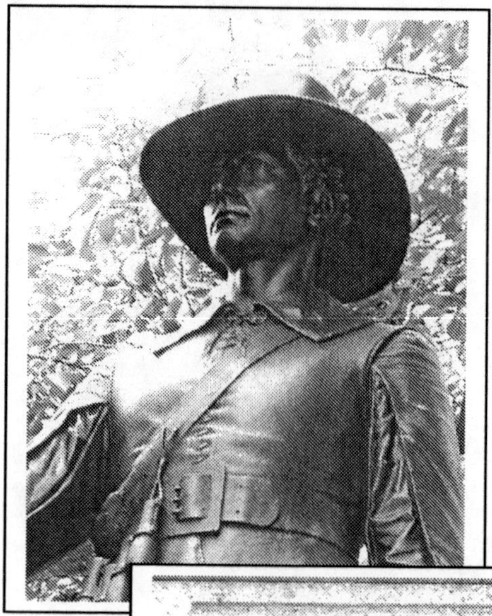

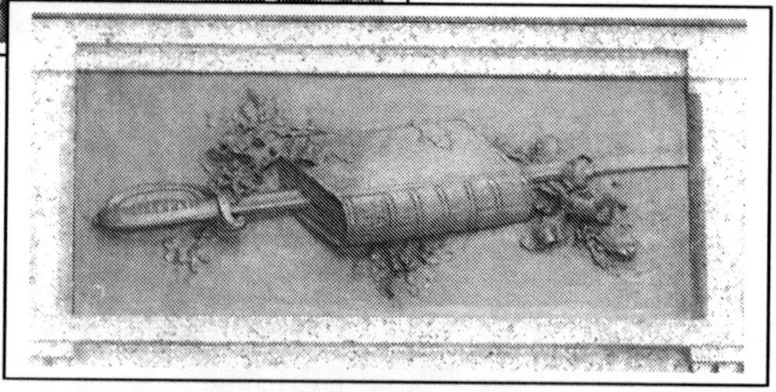

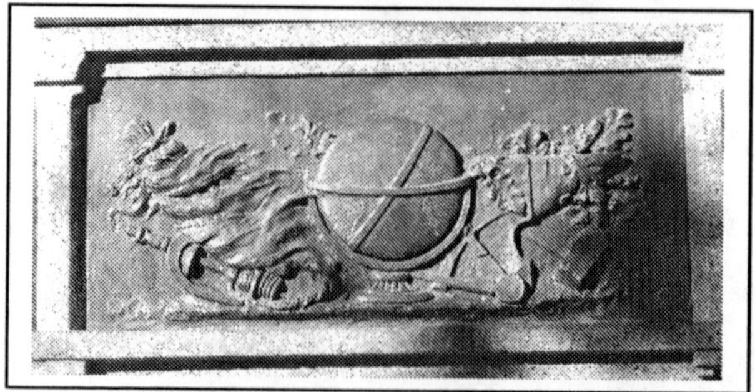

Photos © Dianne L. Durante

Photo © Dianne L. Durante

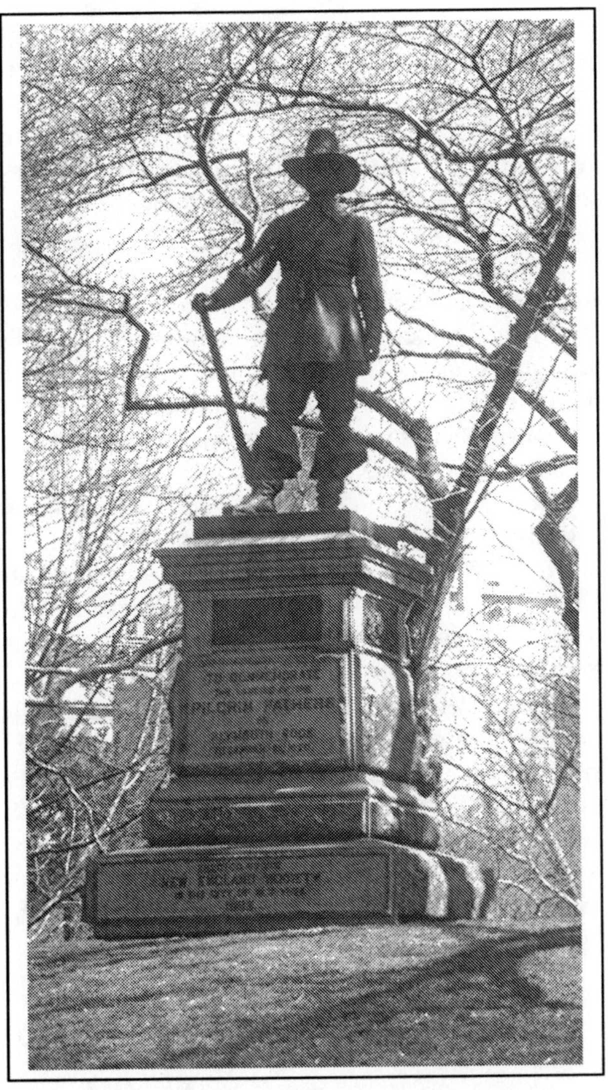

sword. According to Reynolds, this symbolizes the sharp insights to be found in the Bible. The relief on the Pilgrim's left (the south side) incorporates a globe, a sextant for navigation, a hammer and anvil, and a spindle with yarn. On the relief behind the *Pilgrim*, the *Mayflower* sweeps along, all sails set. The fourth relief shows a bow and a quiver full of arrows. Together these images evoke not only religion—the trait we most often associate with the New England settlers—but technology, commerce, and martial courage. (Now that you've cut your teeth on the details of the *Columbus Monument,* consider the change in emphasis here if these reliefs were rearranged, for instance with the bow and arrows on the front.)

The difference between Ward's *Pilgrim* and Saint Gaudens' *Puritan* most likely stems less from the personal beliefs of Ward and Saint Gaudens than from the purpose for which each sculpture was designed. Saint Gaudens' *Puritan* was privately commissioned by a descendant of one of the three Puritan founders of Springfield, a man influential in the early government and church of Massachusetts.

Ward's statue, on the other hand, was commissioned for the seventy-fifth anniversary of the New England Society, founded in 1805 by New-England merchants who had migrated to New York. The Society's annual celebration of the Pilgrims' landing was one of the most glittering events on nineteenth-century New York's social calendar. Why did the New England Society erect a statue? Perhaps because, amid a flood of late-nineteenth-century immigration from Eastern and Southern Europe, the *Pilgrim* served as a visual reminder that the English were here first. England, asserted orator George William Curtis at the statue's dedication, was "the mother country of our distinctive America, the mother of our language and its literature, of our characteristic national impulse, and of the great muniments of our individual liberty."

"Landing of the Pilgrim Fathers"

The breaking waves dashed high,
On a stern and rock-bound coast,
And the woods against a stormy sky,
Their giant branches tossed;

And the heavy night hung dark,
The hills and waters o'er,
When a band of exiles moored their bark
On the wild New England shore.

Not as the conqueror comes,
They, the true-hearted came;
Not with the roll of the stirring drums,
And the trumpet that sings of fame;

Not as the flying come,
In silence and in fear—
They shook the depths of the desert gloom
With their hymns of lofty cheer.

Amidst the storm they sang,
And the stars heard, and the sea;
And the sounding aisles of the dim woods rang
To the anthem of the free.

The ocean eagle soared
From his nest by the white wave's foam;
And the rocking pines of the forest roared—
This was their welcome home.

There were men with hoary hair
Amidst that pilgrim band:
Why had they come to wither there,
Away from their childhood's land?

There was a woman's fearless eye,
Lit by her deep love's truth;
There was manhood's brow serenely high,
And the fiery heart of youth.

What sought they thus afar?
Bright jewels of the mine?
The wealth of seas, the spoils of war?
They sought a faith's pure shrine!

Aye, call it holy ground,
The soil where first they trod;
They have left unstained what there they found—
Freedom to worship God.
—Felicia Hemans (d. 1835)

About the subject

At the dedication of Ward's *Pilgrim*, a choir sang Hemans' "Landing of the Pilgrim Fathers" (see sidebar), which concludes:

> Aye, call it holy ground,
> The soil where first they trod;
> They have left unstained what there they found—
> Freedom to worship God.

Fleeing persecution in Anglican England, then fleeing the mundane but distracting comforts of the Netherlands, the Pilgrims showed tremendous determination and courage in seeking a place to worship as they believed proper. During the 1620-1621 New England winter they suffered appalling losses:

> In two or three months' time half of their company died, especially in January and February, being the depth of winter, and wanting houses and other comforts; being infected with the scurvy and other diseases, which the long voyage and their inaccommodate condition had brought upon them; so as there died sometimes two or three a day, in the foresaid time; that of 100 and odd persons, scarce 50 remained. (William Bradford)

Yet the religious settlers of Massachusetts persisted, and created a colony significantly different from other early-seventeenth-century European settlements in North America.

In Quebec, the French built a fort and trading post manned by a few soldiers. The English at Jamestown, Virginia established a small, fortified settlement primarily to repel Indians while they sought gold. The Pilgrims were the first Europeans to bring families to North America, intending to settle permanently. In that sense, the Pilgrims played a fundamental role in what became the United States.

In an intellectual sense, however, they were not fundamental. The Pilgrims did not permit freedom of worship within their colony. In the early years, punishment for disagreeing with the established religion was harsh: at a 1637 Assembly,

> The erroneous opinions, which were spread in the country, were read (being eighty in all); next the unwholesome expressions; then the scriptures abused. ... There were about eighty opinions, some blasphemous, others erroneous, and all unsafe, condemned by the whole assembly ... Upon this some of Boston departed from the assembly, and came no more. (John Winthrop)

To the Puritans, the First Amendment's statement that "Congress shall make no law respecting an establishment of religion, or prohibiting free exercise thereof" would have been anathema. The idea of religious toleration—true "freedom to worship God" (or not to worship)—came to the Founding Fathers from eighteenth-century Enlightenment philosophy, which was overwhelmingly secular.

Bibliography and further reading

On the statue and its dedication, see *New York Times* articles of 4/14/1884 and 6/7/1885. Stokes 5:1988. Gayle & Cohen p. 220. Reynolds p. 66. SIRIS control #IAS 87870161. Saint Gaudens' full-size *Puritan* in Springfield is SIRIS control #AIS 77000790. His *Pilgrim*, a slight variation on the *Puritan*, stands in Fairmount Park, Philadelphia. The Metropolitan Museum of Art and many other museums have reduced-size casts of the *Puritan*.

Extensive quotes from Bradford, Winthrop and other early Massachusetts settlers appear in T.J. Stiles, ed., *In Their Own Words: The Colonizers* (New York, 1998), Chapters 5, 6 and 9. On the New England Society, see Burrows and Wallace, *Gotham*, pp. 337, 454-5. On the philosophies of the Pilgrims and the Virginians, see John Ridpath, "Virginia and the Virginians," and Eric Daniels, "History of America: Prelude to Revolution, 1607-1763," both audiotapes available through the Ayn Rand Bookstore. On immigration, see Essays Number 14 and 15 on *The Immigrants* and *The Garment Worker*.

Provenance

The inscription reads, "To commemorate the landing of the Pilgrim Fathers on Plymouth Rock, December 21, 1620. Erected by the New

England Society of the City of New York, 1885." Collection of the City of New York.

Essay Number 5

1799

Alexander von Humboldt

Knowledge and comprehension are the joy and justification of humanity. —Humboldt

Artist: Gustaf Blaeser

Dedicated: 1869

Medium and size: Bronze bust (5 feet), granite pedestal (9 feet).

Location: Central Park West at 77th Street, just east of the Museum of Natural History. The statue faces west, and is best seen in the afternoon.

About the statue

Serious expression, broad face, high, thoughtful forehead: a reclusive professor, you'd think, not a man who spent years exploring the wilderness of South America by canoe, on foot and on mule back. Only the wavy hair gives him an energetic look. (Imagine him with slicked-back hair and you'll realize the importance of this feature.) Humboldt is a mature man, with some lines on his face even though he's not frowning or smiling, and his age gives him an air of authority. But it is the eyes that strike one most: open and focused, with the look of someone accustomed to observing and evaluating facts.

Intelligent, thoughtful, energetic, willing to look reality in the face: what more appropriate qualities could one require of an explorer?

Enlightenment View of Knowledge

Man cannot have an effect on nature, cannot adopt any of her forces, if he does not know the natural laws in terms of measurement and numerical relations. Here also lies the strength of the natural intelligence, which increases and decreases according to such knowledge. Knowledge and comprehension are the joy and justification of humanity; they are parts of the national wealth, often a replacement for those materials that nature has all too sparsely dispensed. Those very peoples who are behind in general industrial activity, in application of mechanics and technical chemistry, in careful selection and processing of natural materials, such that regard for such enterprise does not permeate all classes, will inevitably decline in prosperity; all the more so where neighboring states, in which science and the industrial arts have an active interrelationship, progress with youthful vigor.

—Humboldt, *Cosmos* (1845-1862)

About the subject

Starting in 1799, Humboldt (1769-1859) faced ravenous insects, blizzards, typhoid fever, dysentery, floods, thunderstorms, earthquakes, jaguars, and fish with enough voltage to kill a horse as he and French naturalist Aimé Bonpland set out on the first meticulous and extensive scientific exploration of Central and South America. When they sailed home five years later, they had investigated the Venezuelan coast, the Amazon and Orinoco Rivers, the Andes Mountains, and parts of present-day Peru,

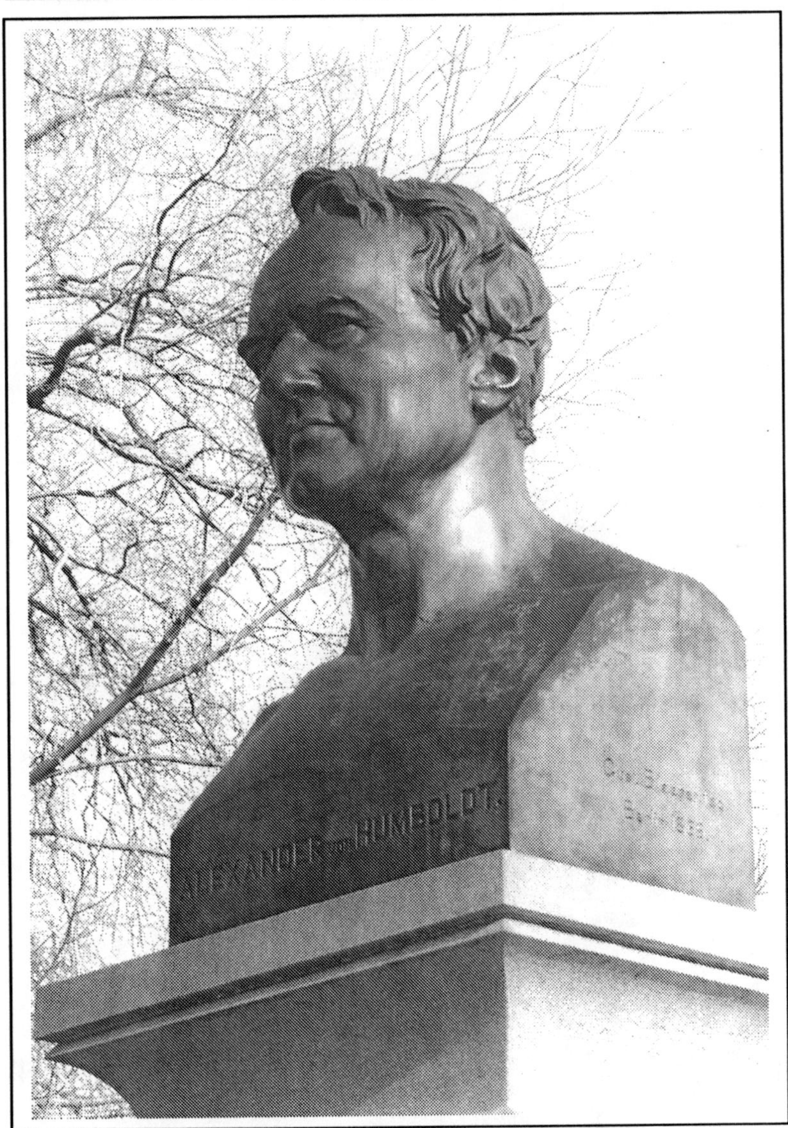

Photo © Dianne L. Durante

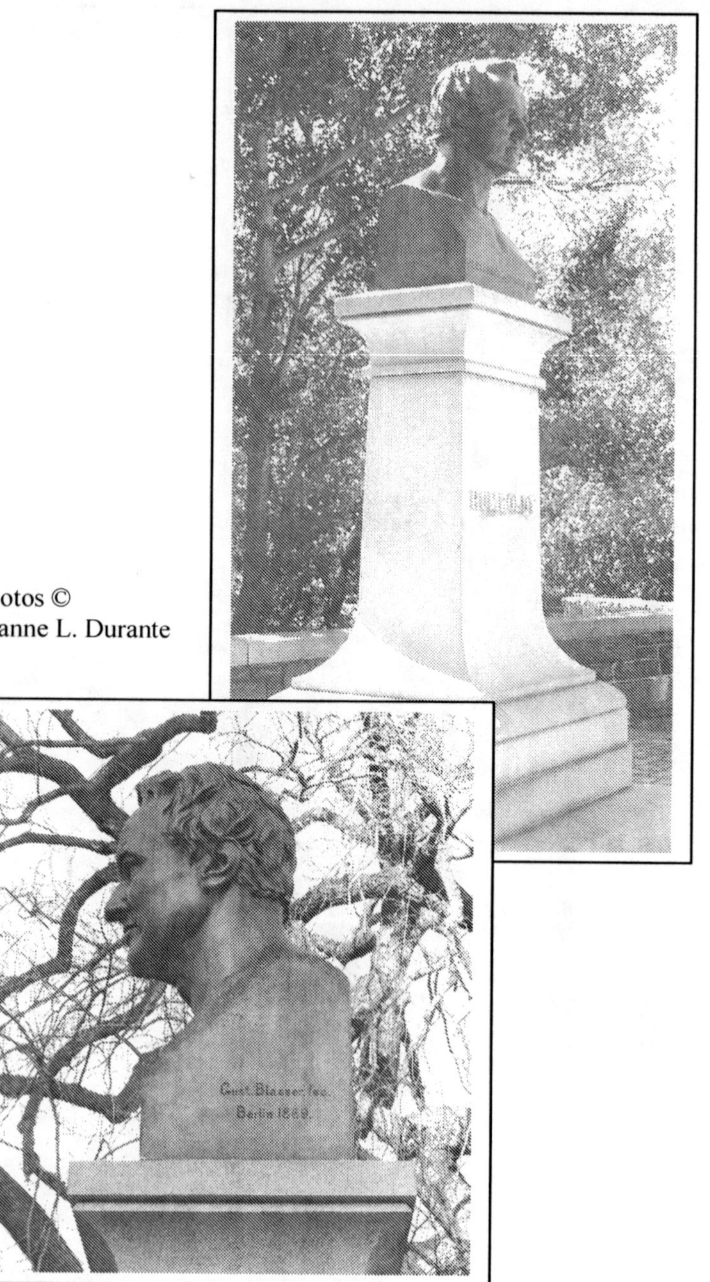

Photos ©
Dianne L. Durante

Ecuador, Colombia and Mexico. The two researchers gathered some 60,000 specimens of rocks and plants while taking copious notes on volcanoes, ocean currents, the earth's magnetism, climate and animal life. Humboldt's 30-volume report on the expedition was one of the few works Darwin packed for his historic voyage on the *Beagle* in the 1830s.

Humboldt is an outstanding exponent of the Enlightenment quest for knowledge that drove scientists to the ends of the earth. Meteorologist, botanist, geologist, geographer and oceanographer, his widespread influence was eulogized by a colleague:

> If we read Barth on Central Africa, we find Humboldt; if we read Say's *Political Economy*, we find his name; if we study the history of the Nineteenth Century, we find his name in the diplomacy of Prussia and France; if we read general literature we find his name in connection with Schiller and Madame de Stael; if we look at modern maps we find his isothermal lines; if we consult Grim's *Dictionary of the German Language* we find Humboldt as authority. (Prof. Lieber, *New York Times* 6/3/1859)

Humboldt's urge to integrate knowledge into an all-embracing view of the physical universe is exemplified in his five-volume *Cosmos*, published 1845-1862, near the end of a career that spanned two-thirds of a century. (See sidebar for an excerpt.) Humboldt knew Goethe and Schiller, reported on his American expedition to President Thomas Jefferson, and was lauded by Simon Bolivar: "Humboldt has done more good for America than all her conquerors." Indeed, his reports prompted a plethora of scholarly studies on the history and discovery of the Americas, as well as their economics and politics. His 1799 expedition has aptly been dubbed "the scientific discovery of America."

Bibliography and further reading

Gayle & Cohen p. 245. SIRIS control #IAS 76008978.

The *New York Times* printed several eulogies of Humboldt on 6/3/1859. For a very readable description of Humboldt's expedition to South America, see David McCullough, "Journey to the Top of the World," Ch. 1 in *Brave Companions: Portraits in History*. On Humboldt's importance as a scientist, see Kurt-R. Biermann, "Alexander von Humboldt," *Dictionary of Scientific Biography* VI, 549-55. Detailed biographies with bibliographies also appear in "Alexander von Humboldt," *World of Scientific Discovery*, 2nd ed., Gale Group, 1999 (reproduced in Biography Resource Center, Farmington Hills, Mich.: The Gale Group, 2002, http://www.galenet. com/servlet/BioRC, Document No. K1648000341), and "Alexander von Humboldt," *Explorers and Discoverers of the World*, Gale Research, 1993 (reproduced in Biography Resource Center, Farmington Hills, Mich.: The Gale Group, 2002, http://www.galenet.com/servlet/ BioRC, Document Number: K1614000155).

Manhattan has statues of Humboldt's acquaintances Goethe, Schiller, Jefferson and Bolivar: see forthcoming Forgotten Delights volumes on artists (for the first two), on politicians and on defenders.

Provenance

Inscription on the base of the bronze bust: "Alexander von Humboldt"; on the side, "Gustav Blaeser fec[it], Berlin 1869." On the pedestal: "Humboldt." Proposed by the Geographical Society and funded by the Humboldt Memorial Association, the bust was originally placed at 59th Street and Fifth Avenue. In 1981 it was moved to its present location, appropriately facing the American Museum of Natural History. The base appears to be unchanged—not always the case when a sculpture is moved. Collection of the City of New York.

Essay Number 6

1830

Peter Cooper

The success of this locomotive ... answered the question of the possibility of building railroads in a country scarce of capital, and with immense stretches of very rough country to pass, in order to connect commercial centers ...
—Cooper

Artist: Augustus Saint Gaudens

Dedicated: 1894

Medium and size: Bronze, over life-size. Granite pedestal, canopy and columns with pink marble backdrop by Stanford White. Overall 20 feet high, 18 feet wide, 10.5 feet deep.

Location: Cooper Square south of the Cooper Union, where the Bowery splits into Third and Fourth Avenues. The statue faces south, and is well lit at most times of day.

About the statue

If Moses were a grandfather, he'd look like this: dignified, authoritative and energetic, but still approachable. The authority comes from the lined face and full beard, reminiscent of an Old-Testament prophet's. (Michelangelo's *Moses* and Donatello's *St. John the Evangelist* come to mind.) But rather than a prophet's flowing robes, *Cooper* wears the frock coat of a well-to-do nineteenth-century gentleman. His feet are on the ground, one slightly ahead of the other, as if he's ready to rise with the assistance of his elegant cane.

Cooper could easily have appeared aloof and regal: imagine the arms and legs positioned with rigid symmetry, and the cane elaborate enough to be scepter-like. As it is, the pose's faint resemblance to portraits of medieval kings or Byzantine mosaics of Christ in Majesty gives the *Cooper* a trace of grandeur, while the slight relaxation and modern dress make him approachable.

Saint Gaudens contrasts the smoothness of *Cooper's* face with the roughness of the beard and hair, and the texture of his clothing with the polish of the chair. Such contrasts may seem an obvious way to focus attention, but seldom are they used so expertly. In late twentieth-century sculpture, they're often abandoned completely: see, for example, the texture of *The Immigrants*, later in this volume.

The size and pose of the *Cooper* make it impressive, but Saint Gaudens collaborated with architect Stanford White to make it even more so. White designed an elaborate granite-and-marble "frame" against which the bronze stands out vividly. The style of letters and numerals on the pedestal's inscription evokes the grandeur and dignity of the Romans—a favorite technique among artists and sculptors from the Middle Ages on, and one particularly favored by Neoclassical artists of the nineteenth century.

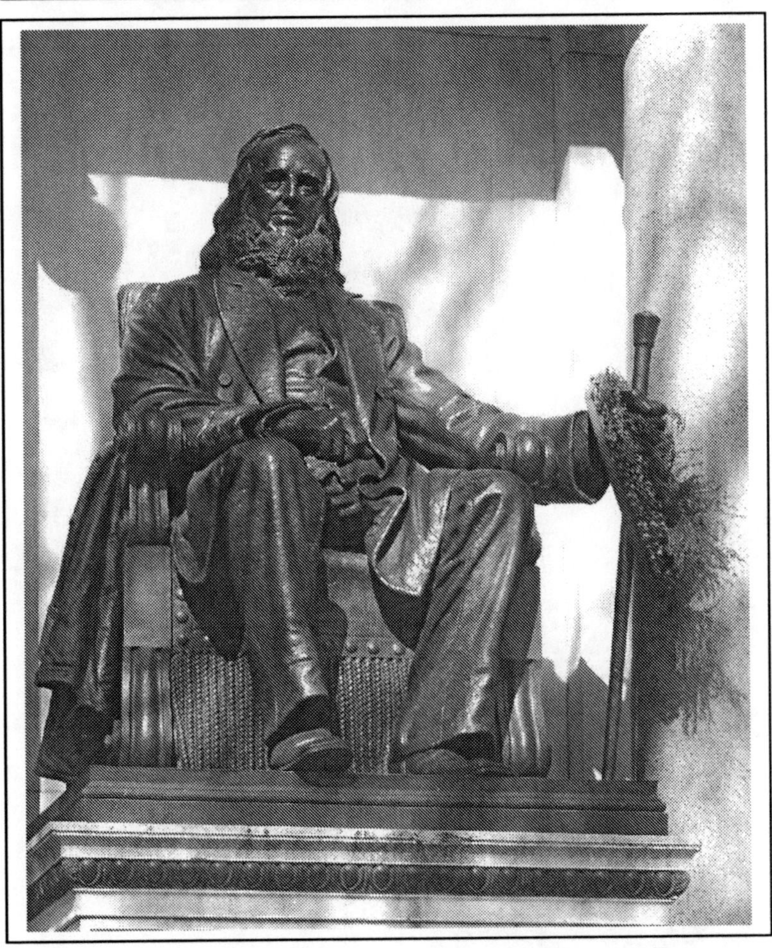

Photo © Dianne L. Durante. NOTE: The wreath hanging on *Cooper's* cane is not part of the sculpture.

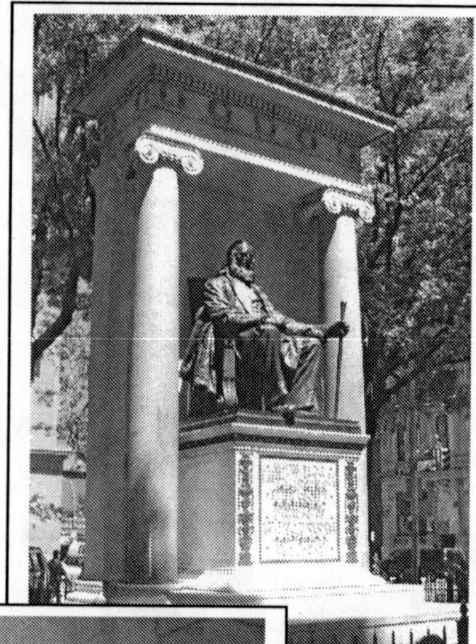

Photos ©
Dianne L. Durante

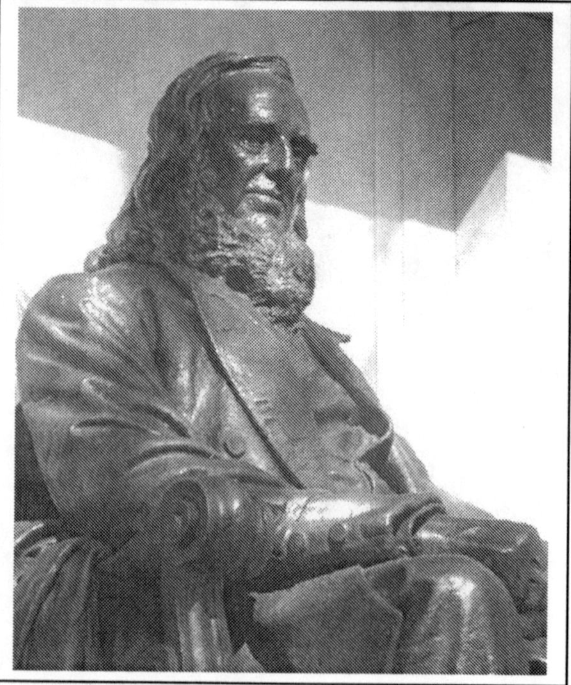

Cooper on America's First Working Steam Locomotive

When we first purchased the property [in Baltimore] it was in the midst of a great excitement created by a promise of the rapid completion of the Baltimore & Ohio Railroad, which had been commenced by a subscription of five dollars per share. In the course of the first year's operations they had spent more than the five dollars per share. But the road had to make so many short turns in going around points of rocks that they found they could not complete the road without a much larger sum than they had supposed would be necessary; while the many short turns in the road seemed to render it entirely useless for locomotive purposes. The principal stockholders had become so discouraged that they said, they would not pay any more, and would lose all they had already paid in. After conversing with them, I told them that if they would hold on a little while, I would put a small locomotive on the road, which I thought would demonstrate the practicability of using steam-engines on the road, even with all the short turns in it. I got up a small engine for that purpose, and put it on the road, and invited the stockholders to witness the experiment. After a great deal of trouble and difficulty in accomplishing the work, the stockholders came, and thirty-six men were taken into a car, and, with six men on the locomotive, which carried its own fuel and water, and having to go up hill eighteen feet to a mile, and turn all the short turns around the points of rocks, we succeeded in making the thirteen miles, on the first passage out, in one hour and twelve minutes; and we returned from Ellicott's Mills to Baltimore in fifty-seven minutes.

This locomotive was built to demonstrate that cars could be drawn around short curves, beyond anything believed in at that time to be possible. The success of this locomotive also answered the question of the possibility of building railroads in a country scarce of capital, and with immense stretches of very rough country to pass, in order to connect commercial centers, without the deep cuts, the tunneling, and leveling which short curves might avoid. My contrivance saved this road from bankruptcy.

—Cooper, *Sketch of the Early Days of Peter Cooper*, 1877 (pp. 5-6)

About the subject

As the Industrial Revolution gathered momentum in America during the early years of the nineteenth century, Cooper (1791-1883) demonstrated the innovation and flexibility that made him one of the wealthiest businessmen of his time. He improved the cloth-shearing machine of an early employer and bought the rights to market it. He ran a retail grocery business and invested in New York real estate. In 1821 his high-quality, reasonably priced glue began to displace imported European glues on the American market.

Then, in 1828, Cooper was duped into becoming sole owner of a three-mile stretch of Baltimore waterfront. Struggling to compete commercially with Boston, Philadelphia and New York, the citizens of Baltimore planned to build a railroad to connect their harbor with Ohio, on the American frontier. Cooper's land, rich in iron ore and at the terminus of the Baltimore and Ohio Railroad (yes, the one on the Monopoly board), would be extremely valuable once the B&O was operating.

Alas, the B&O was not. Designed for horse-drawn carriages, the tracks wound in tight curves through the rolling hills of Maryland. When George Stephenson introduced the steam locomotive in England in the late 1820s, the B&O wanted to purchase one for its own use—but Stephenson's locomotive could not negotiate the curves laid down in Maryland. The owners and engineers were stumped. The investors refused to provide more funds. By 1830 the B&O Railroad faced bankruptcy, and Cooper faced a precipitous drop in the value of his Baltimore property.

Cooper, an inveterate tinkerer, cobbled together a locomotive with a shorter wheelbase and smaller wheels than Stephenson's model. The engine, later nicknamed "Tom Thumb," first ran on the B&O's convoluted tracks in 1830. Although it was so slow that it once lost a race to a horse, it was the first successful steam locomotive built in America. Cooper points out in his autobiography (see sidebar) that the "Tom Thumb" made the future development of railroads in the United States feasible by demonstrating that railroad tracks could be built without the expensive tunneling necessary to keep rails running level and straight.

The railroads were crucial to America's development. They moved passengers and freight rapidly and inexpensively. They lowered costs and spurred heavy industry and large-scale manufacturing. They spawned new methods of corporate financing. "No invention in history had so swift and decisive an effect upon the world economy as did the railroad," asserts Gordon. "Indeed, it might almost be said that the railroad created the world economy out of a myriad of local ones." (*The Great Game*, p. 75)

Cooper soon sold his Baltimore property and opened an iron-manufacturing plant on Thirty-Third Street in Manhattan, and then a larger one in Trenton, New Jersey. A leader in the American iron trade, his company produced rails for the burgeoning railroad industry (including the B&O) and cables for telegraphs and suspension bridges. The Trenton factory also manufactured the world's first I-beams. "Fireproof buildings" constructed with them were a boon to New York (where devastating fires still destroyed hundreds of buildings at a time), and were the predecessors of the modern skyscraper.

Although Cooper's successes and innovations ranged from the I-beam and the "Tom Thumb" to powdered gelatin (hello, Jell-o!), in his entire life Cooper only attended school for 52 days. He felt strongly that had he been better educated, he would have wasted less time trying to implement ideas that were physically impossible. So when Cooper was in his 60s, he used his own money to establish the Cooper Union for the Advancement of Science and Art. The Union offered free evening courses to thousands of working-class New Yorkers. "Its aim—to help young men and women to train their faculties to sound and thorough work while preserving their self-reliance and awakening genuine ambition—has been pursued with skill and energy and patience and great success" (*New York Times* 5/29/1897). Augustus Saint Gaudens, who sculpted *Cooper*, was one of the Union's earliest and most illustrious pupils (class of 1864), studying drawing there while he worked as a cameo-cutter.

The Cooper Union's home, which still stands on Fourth Avenue at the Bowery, was New York's first fireproof building, and at seven stories its tallest. The Union's Great Hall was the scene of speeches by Ulysses S. Grant, Theodore Roosevelt, Susan B. Anthony and Frederick Douglass, as well the "Right Makes Might" speech (2/27/1860) that established Abraham Lincoln's anti-slavery platform.

Bibliography and further reading

On the statue, see *New York Times* 5/29/1897, 5/30/1897. Gayle & Cohen p. 83. SIRIS control #IAS 76003477.

On Cooper, see *A Sketch of the Early Days and Business Life of Peter Cooper. An Autobiography* (1877), and Edward L. Lach, Jr., "Cooper, Peter" (http://www.anb.org/articles/10/10-00328.html; American National Biography Online Feb. 2000, with bibliography). For contemporary comments on Cooper, see *New York Times* obituaries and accounts of Cooper's funeral, 4/5/1883, 4/6/1883, 4/8/1883; also Russell Edwards, "Peter Cooper: Citizen and Benefactor of New York," *New York Times* 6/5/1966. For Cooper's participation in the Transatlantic Cable, see Essay Number 7 on Morse.

For a good short summary of the progress of the railroads in the United States, see John Steele Gordon, *The Great Game: A History of Wall Street* (1999), pp. 73-78. For the railroads in New York, see Burrows and Wallace, *Gotham* pp. 563-69 and elsewhere. For more on all phases of railroads in the nineteenth century, see *The Encyclopedia of American Business History and Biography: Railroads in the Nineteenth Century,* ed. Robert L. Frey (New York and Oxford, 1988). On Saint Gaudens, one of America's greatest sculptors, see Burke Wilkinson, *Uncommon Clay: The Life and Works of Augustus Saint Gaudens*, and John F. Dryfhout, *The Work of Augustus Saint Gaudens.*

On Lincoln, see the forthcoming Forgotten Delights volume on politicians.

Provenance

The inscription on the front of the pedestal reads, "Erected by the citizens of New York in grateful remembrance of Peter Cooper, founder of the Cooper Union for the Advancement of Science and Art. Anno Domini MDCCC XCVII." On the back: "Peter Cooper, born February XII A.D. MDCCXCI, died April III A.D. MDCCCLXXXIII." A public subscription raised $39,000 for the statue, whose cost was $25,000 (a substantial price for the time); the remaining funds were used to beautify the park in which the *Cooper* sits. Collection of the City of New York.

Essay Number 7

1843

Samuel Finley Breese Morse

.. –. ...– . –. – –– .–.

–– ..–.

–– –– .–. ... .

–.–. –– –.. .

(Inventor of Morse Code)

> Artist: Byron M. Pickett
>
> Dedicated: 1870
>
> Medium and size: Bronze statue (8 feet), granite pedestal (6.5 feet).
>
> Location: Just inside Central Park at 72nd Street (near Fifth Avenue). It faces north but is surrounded by trees: best viewed at mid-day or later, and after the leaves have fallen.

About the statue

Pickett's *Morse* is not, by any standard, as attractive as Michelangelo's *David*. In fact, few portrait sculptures delight us with their beauty. But that's not their purpose. As Bryant explains (see sidebar), the purpose of portraits is to remind us of great deeds and great minds—of what the best among us have accomplished and of the heights to which each of us can aspire.

To achieve this purpose, a portraitist must be selective: he must create a strong physical resemblance and show the sitter in a characteristic attitude. Morse—who was still alive when this statue was dedicated—is represented as an alert, authoritative elderly man. Looking far into the distance, he rests his left hand on a model of the telegraph while his right holds a tickertape printout. The long flowing beard gives him the same Old-Testament authority we saw in *Peter Cooper.* (The *Cooper* was executed 24 years later: it appears earlier in this volume of Forgotten Delights because Cooper's excursion into railroads was earlier than Morse's telegraph.)

Morse wears a toga-like cape and stands next to an ancient Doric-style column that supports the highest technology of the time: a telegraph. This juxtaposition of ancient with high-tech is typical of nineteenth-century America, when industry was making great strides but Greek and Roman details were still thought to convey an air of dignity and permanence.

A *New York Times* reporter examining the yet-to-be-assembled *Morse* statue at the foundry noted approvingly,

> There is no disgusting attempt at cheap realism in buttons or boots or cravat, as happens occasionally in such works, and the sculptor has thrown all his power into the pose of the body, the arrangement of the arms and the expression of the face.

Although resemblance to the sitter and a characteristic attitude are required for a portrait, extremes of minute detail are not. We will return to the question of detail when looking at *The Immigrants*.

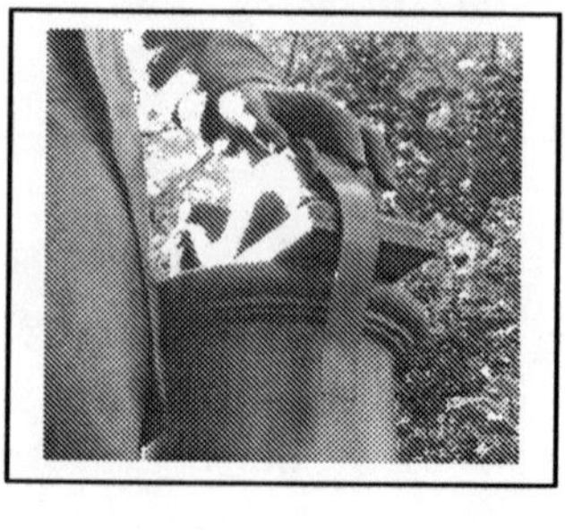

Photo © Dianne L. Durante

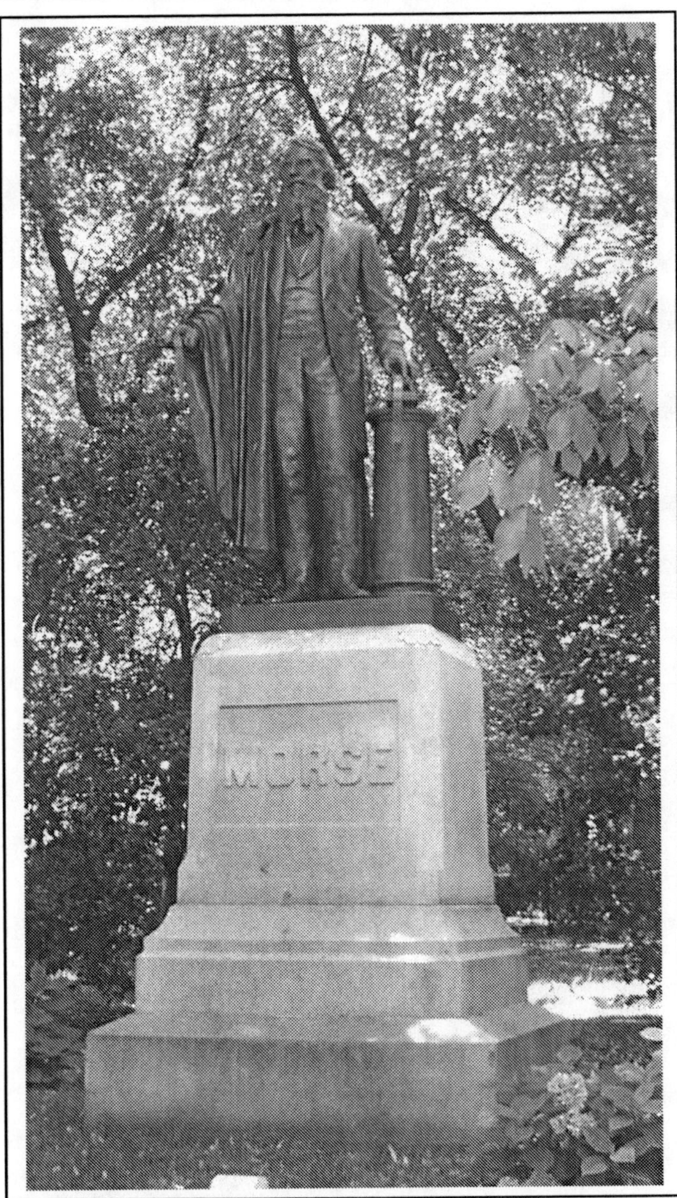

Photo © Dianne L. Durante

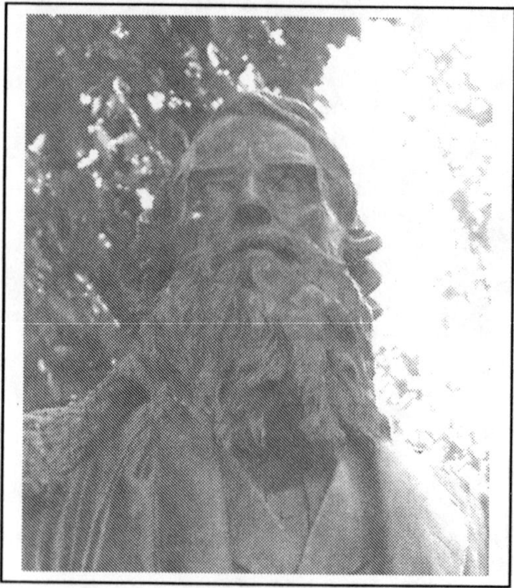

Photo © Dianne L. Durante

William Cullen Bryant on Portrait Statues

It may be said, I know, that the civilized world is already full of memorials which speak the merit of our friend, and the grandeur and utility of his invention. Every telegraphic station is such a memorial; every message sent from one of these stations to another may be counted among the honors paid to his name. Every telegraphic wire strung from post to post, as it hums in the wind, murmurs his eulogy. Every sheaf of wires laid down in the deep sea, occupying the bottom of soundless abysses, to which human sight has never penetrated, and carrying the electric pulse, charged with the burden of human thought from continent to continent, from the Old World to the New, is a testimonial to his greatness. ... [Yet] we are so constituted that we insist upon seeing the form of that brow beneath which an active, restless, creative brain devised the mechanism that was to subdue the most wayward of the elements to the service of man and make it his obedient messenger. We require to see the eye that glittered with a thousand lofty hopes, when the great discovery was made, and the lips that curled with a smile of triumph when it became certain that the lightning of the clouds would become tractable to the most delicate touch. We demand to see the hand which first strung the wire by whose means the slender currents of the electric fluid were taught the alphabet of every living language—the hand which pointed them to the spot where they were to inscribe and leave their messages. All this we have in the statue which has this day been unveiled to the eager gaze of the public.

—William Cullen Bryant at the unveiling of the *Morse* statue, June 1871

About the subject

In the late 1830s, "Since for all practical purposes news could travel no faster than human beings could carry it, knowledge of events in Europe—the center of the Western world—was just as slow to flow across the ocean as men and goods. North America was not only three thousand miles from Europe—it was two months from it as well." (Gordon, *Thread Across the Ocean*, p. 3.) Early machines for long-distance communication via electrical impulses were complex and unreliable. One primitive telegraph employed a separate wire for each letter of the alphabet, each connected to a bell with a different sound. Another produced an EKG-like printout that was exceptionally difficult to decipher.

Morse (1791-1872) was an unlikely candidate to change the face of worldwide communication. One of a mere handful of prominent American painters, he produced portraits of the Marquis de Lafayette, James Monroe, DeWitt Clinton, William Cullen Bryant and others. But like many an artist, he found painting financially unprofitable. Perhaps for that reason he began to experiment with the telegraph while eking out a living as a New York University professor in the 1830s.

Working with two more technically knowledgeable colleagues, Morse succeeded in reducing the number of wires in a telegraph to one, and in developing a code that allowed easy transmission while permitting trained operators to "hear" messages as they were being transmitted, rather than waiting for a print-out. Although Morse is sometimes portrayed as a dilettante dabbling in science, no dilettante could have focused on the telegraph for the long years it took Morse to develop his code, build a working telegraph line and oversee the invention's development and distribution until it turned a profit.

Congress appropriated $30,000 for a telegraph line from Baltimore to Washington in 1843 (it was strung in the right-of-way of the B&O Railroad), but declined to purchase the rights to the equipment. Morse instead licensed the telegraph for use across America, earning hundreds of thousands of dollars.

> The telegraph was something very new under the sun, something that would have been utterly inconceivable to the [eighteenth-century] world... The telegraph could transmit information at very high speed—thousands of times faster than it could be physically carried and hundreds of times faster than Chappe's visual telegraph could transmit it—and at very low cost. So it is not surprising that once its practicality was demonstrated, the telegraph spread with astonishing speed, often using the convenient pathways forged by the equally fast-spreading railroads. (Gordon, *Thread* p. 9)

By 1854, 23,000 miles of telegraph wires stretched across the United States.

The network of telegraph wires transmitted an unexpected bonus to New York. With communication nearly instantaneous across the United States, Wall Street became the nation's financial capital, making regional stock markets in Philadelphia and Boston obsolete. (See Gordon, *The Great Game*, pp. 80-81.)

Bibliography and further reading

On the sculpture, see *New York Times* articles of 6/7/1871 and 6/11/1871. Gayle & Cohen p. 210. SIRIS control #IAS 76003533.

On Morse, see Samuel Irenaeus Prime, *The Life of Samuel F.B. Morse, Inventor of the Electro-Magnetic Recording Telegraph* (New York, 1875); and Bernard S. Finn, "Morse, Samuel Finley Breese" (http://www.anb.org/articles/13/13-01183.html; American National Biography Online Feb. 2000, with bibliography). See also George H. Drury, "Samuel F.B. Morse," in *Encyclopedia of American Business History and Biography: Railroads in the Nineteenth Century*, ed. Robert L. Frey (New York and Oxford, 1988), pp. 279-82. Eric Daniels presents a lively short biography of Morse in "The Inventive Age in American History" (audiotape available through The Ayn Rand Bookstore). On the importance of the telegraph and on Morse, see John Steele Gordon, *A Thread Across the Ocean: The Heroic Story of the Transatlantic Cable* (New York, 2002), Chapters 1 and 2.

On the railroads, see the essays in this volume on Cooper, Vanderbilt, Holley and Rea (Numbers 6, 9, 12, 16). On William Cullen Bryant, see the forthcoming Forgotten Delights volume on politicians and media moguls.

Provenance

On the base: "Morse". Funds for this statue were raised by telegraph operators across the country when Morse was 79. He was the last person to have his statue erected in Central Park during his lifetime: in 1873, the Central Park Commissioners ruled that subjects of commemorative sculpture must have been dead at least five years. Collection of the City of New York.

Essay Number 8

1857

Dr. James Marion Sims

"The Father of Gynecology"

Artist: Ferdinand von Miller II

Dedicated: 1892

Medium and size: Bronze (8.75 feet), granite pedestal by Aymar Embury II (12.5 x 6.75 x 2.75 feet).

Location: Central Park at Fifth Avenue and 103rd Street, across from the Academy of Medicine. Faces east; best seen in the morning and when the leaves on the surrounding trees have fallen.

About the statue

With his bowed head, shadowed eyes and solemn mouth, *Dr. Sims* seems to be pondering a diagnosis or deciding how to deliver unpleasant news. Perhaps he has just finished one of the surgeries that made him famous: the overcoat and double-breasted coat beneath it would not have been out of place in an operating room in the 1870s, when sterilization and disinfection were still radically new ideas.

About the subject

In a painting done around the time of the American Revolution, a well-dressed physician comfortably seated in an armchair checks the pulse of a limp white arm. The rest of the woman is modestly concealed behind her bed's velvet curtains. When J. Marion Sims began practicing medicine half a century later, intransigent prudery still precluded male physicians (and all physicians were male) from examining unclothed female patients. Dealing with the female reproductive tract was like performing open-heart surgery blindfolded, and without any idea of what a heart looks like. Women routinely suffered and died from mysterious ailments vaguely referred to as "female complaints."

Sims (1813-1883) began to change that. At a small hospital for women set up in his home in Montgomery, Alabama, he methodically set out to correct the lack of bladder control that often occurred after prolonged and obstructed childbirth. In an era before Depends or even indoor toilets, such incontinence could cause a woman to be a social outcast or an invalid for the rest of her life.

Sims' first contribution to women's health was the invention of an instrument that allowed him to see what he was doing: a silver spoon with its handle bent at a right angle that allowed him to look into the vagina. He later developed this into that indispensable tool of gynecologists, the vaginal speculum. In order to see better during examinations and operations, he had the patient lie on her left side curled into a ball, a position still in use and still known as the "Sims position."

With these aids, Sims determined that the cause of the incontinence was a tear in the wall between the vagina and the bladder, now known as a vesico-vaginal fistula. Then he set out to repair the fistula by stitching the edges together. After numerous failures, Sims discovered that the silk sutures used by contemporary surgeons encouraged infection, and developed the use of

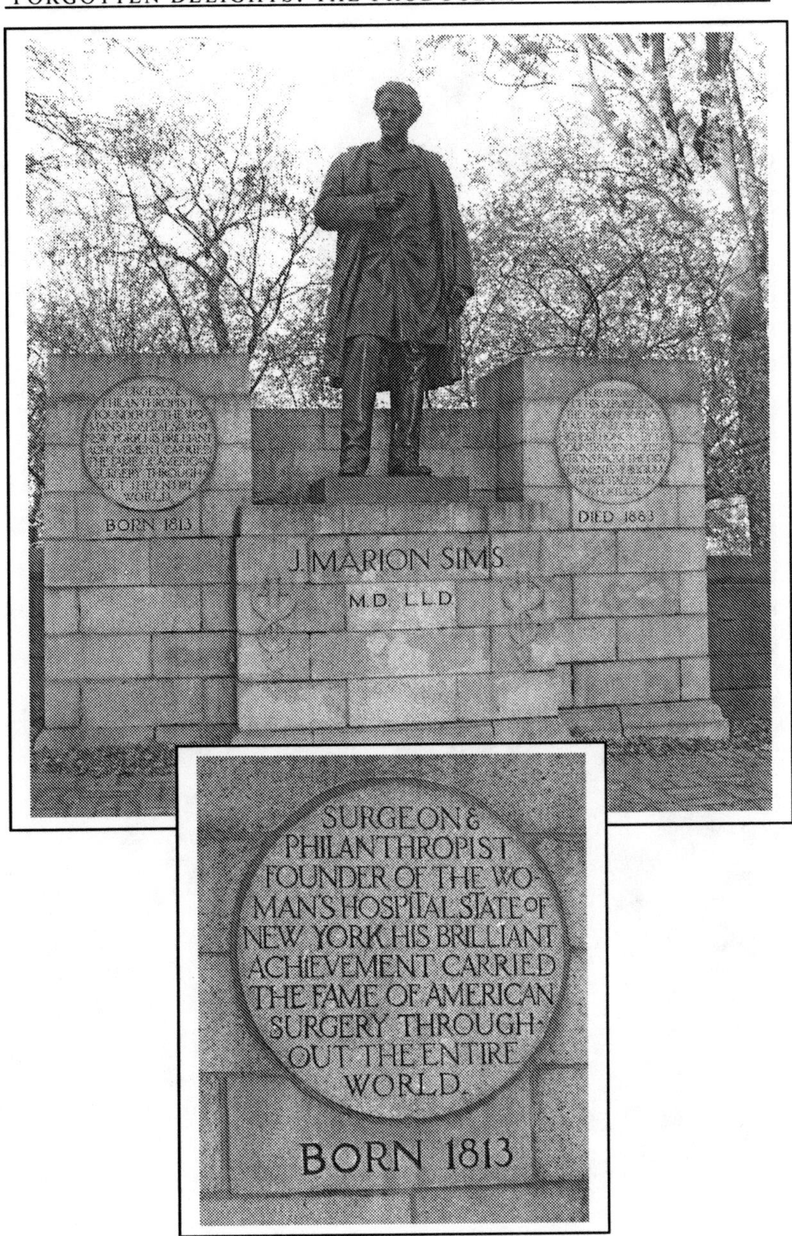

Photos © Dianne L. Durante

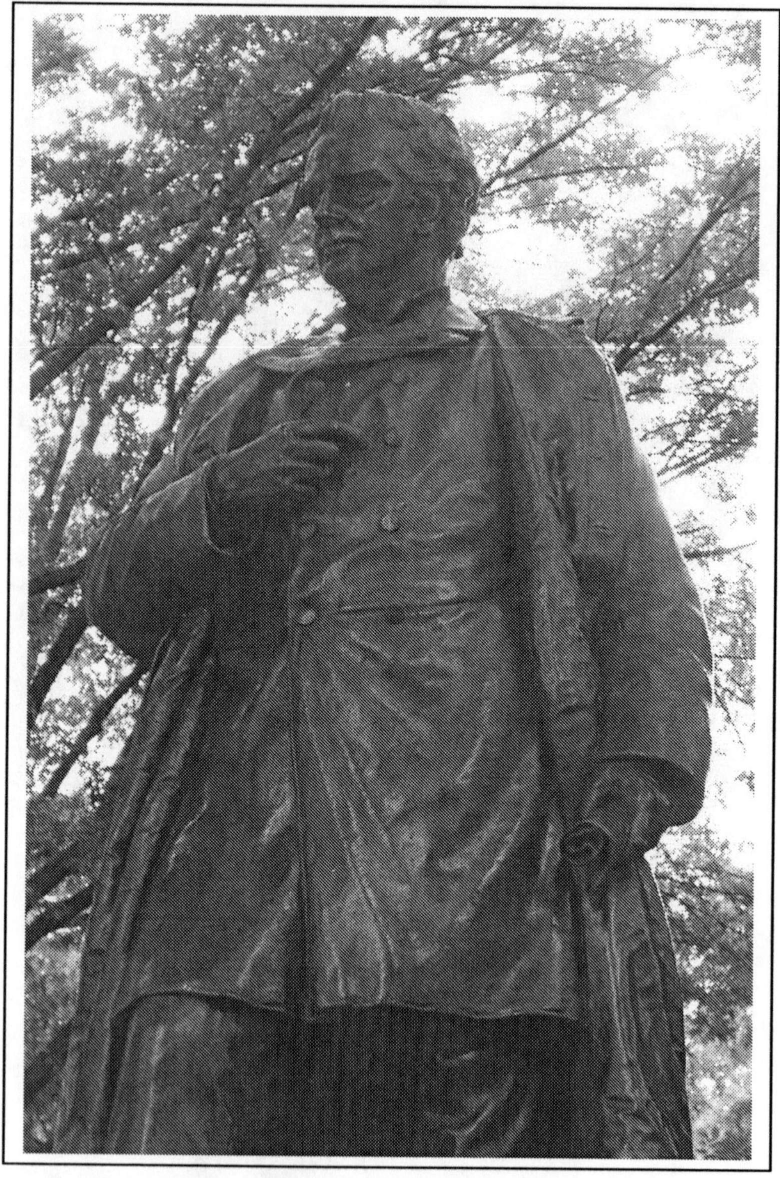

Photo © Dianne L. Durante

silver wire for sutures—a major innovation in surgical procedure.

Sims has been virulently criticized for performing early fistula operations on slaves, whose consent is not recorded anywhere except in Sims' autobiography. On the other hand, recent studies in Africa of vesico-vaginal fistulas indicate that the condition is much more common when a woman is malnourished or bears children very young, both of which were regrettably common among slaves in the United States in the mid-nineteenth century. Sims' efforts improved the lives of some of these slaves in an immediate, concrete way.

Sims moved from Alabama to New York City, there establishing in 1857 the City's first hospital for women. He did it with the backing of a women's philanthropic association: the medical establishment pooh-poohed the need for such a hospital. Self-exiled to Europe during the Civil War because his sympathies lay with his native South, Sims became famous as physician to such prominent women as the wife of Napoleon III. His brilliant (although unsystematic) *Clinical Notes on Uterine Surgery*, 1866, helped gynecology gain recognition as an separate field of medicine and led to surgeons actively intervening in problems of the female reproductive tract, rather than letting nature take its course.

Sims left the Woman's Hospital in 1874 when the Board of Governors made two decisions that showed how far behind the times Board members were. Sims' operations attracted throngs of American and European physicians eager to observe his techniques. Presumably for the sake of the patient's modesty (that old, deadly modesty), the Board decreed that no more than fifteen observers could be present in an operating room.

The Board also forbade the admission to the Hospital of women with uterine cancer, at the time an incurable condition. Since other hospitals also refused admission to such patients, they usually died at home, after months or years of agonizing pain. Sims alleviated this in a minor way by treating cancer patients in a privately run hospital.

Harris, a historian of medicine, sums up Dr. Sims' efforts:

> In the early 1880s, it was a rare person indeed who had not heard of Sims. Not only was he one of America's most famous physicians: he was an international legend, a controversial cosmopolite whose ability to blaze new trails and to effect remarkable cures kept him almost constantly in the limelight and brought him hordes of friends, not a few enemies, and a fabulous income wherever he went—which was practically everywhere.

Man's Proper Heroes

Toward the higher civilization, the progress of man is slow. As yet the shadows of barbarism linger about him. His heroes are the destroyers, the Caesars, the Napoleons, who covered the earth with ruin and buried beneath it countless lives, sacrificed upon the altar of personal ambition. But the time must come when those whose genius and works give life and health and happiness to the world will be first in the heart of man. In this purer temple of fame, along with those of Jenner, Ephraim McDowell, Morton, Lister, Pasteur and others, generations yet unborn shall read the name of Marion Sims.

—John Allan Wyeth, surgeon and Sims' son-in-law (d. 1922; quoted in Sparkman)

Sims made one last major contribution to the improvement of women's health. In October 1883, in a letter to a friend whose offer to fund a cancer pavilion at the Woman's Hospital had been rejected, Sims suggested the establishment of a hospital solely for cancer patients, male and female. In early 1884, a few months after Sims died, the cornerstone was laid for the New York Cancer Hospital's Astor pavilion, dedicated to the treatment of cancer in women. It was the first such hospital in the United States.

I admit that I am more familiar with the careers of Napoleon and Julius Caesar than with those of the scientists and physicians mentioned by Sims' son-in-law (see sidebar): Jenner, McDowell, Morton, Lister, Pasteur. But now, when that postcard arrives reminding me that it's time for my regular gynecological check-up, I think with a smile of Dr. Sims, whose efforts made my life and the lives of countless women longer and healthier.

Bibliography and further reading

On the statue, see *New York Times* articles of 4/7/1887, 10/21/1894, 2/17/1934, 10/21/1934. Gayle & Cohen p. 232. SIRIS control #IAS 76003548.

On Sims, see his autobiography, *The Story of My Life* (1884); Seale Harris, *Woman's Surgeon: The Life Story of J. Marion Sims* (New York, 1950); Robert S. Sparkman, "J. Marion Sims, Woman's Surgeon and More (*Bulletin of the American College of Physicians*, March 1975); and Jane Eliot Sewell, "Sims, J. Marion" (http://www.anb.org/articles/12/12-00851.html; American National Biography Online Feb. 200, with further bibliography).

The painting referred to in "About the Subject" is a portrait of Dr. William Clysson by Winthrop Chandler, in the collection of the Art Institute of Chicago. (See Albert Lyons, *Medicine: An Illustrated History*, p. 467.)

Provenance

On the left side of the present pedestal the inscription reads, "Surgeon and philanthropist, founder of the Woman's Hospital, State of New York. His brilliant achievement carried the fame of American surgery throughout the entire world. Born 1813." On the right the inscription continues, "In recognition of his services in the cause of science and mankind awarded highest honors by his countrymen and decorations from the governments of Belgium, France, Italy, Spain and Portugal. Died 1883." The $10,000 for this statue was donated by 12,000 colleagues and grateful patients, through a subscription organized by the *Medical Record.*

Originally *Sims* stood in Bryant Park, west of the New York Public Library at 42nd Street, on a tall pedestal similar to the one that now holds *Cornelius Vanderbilt*. In 1928 *Sims* and a bust of Washington Irving were moved to make room for a reconstruction of Federal Hall, erected as part of the bicentennial celebration of George Washington's birth. The Parks Department tucked the two bronzes away under the Williamsburg Bridge, where they languished for several years. "Personally," said autocratic Parks Commissioner Robert Moses, "I think the city could get along very well without them, but the Art Commission wants them back and will get them back again." In 1934, following a campaign by influential New York physicians, *Sims* was rededicated opposite the New York Academy of Medicine, with a new base. Collection of the City of New York.

Essay Number 9

1857

Cornelius Vanderbilt

What he bought he bought to keep, to build up, and to make more productive. ... It required skill, patience, and that mental quality which we call forethought, to conduct successfully such vast concerns as those which employed Vanderbilt's energies. —*New York Times*, 1/5/1877

Artist: Ernst Plassman

Dedicated: 1869

Medium and size: Bronze (8.5 feet), granite pedestal (about 8.5 feet).

Location: South facade of Grand Central Terminal, at the level of the Park Avenue viaduct. Pedestrians can enter the Hyatt Hotel (42nd Street just east of Grand Central), go up the stairs on the left to the reception level, go up the escalator to the left of Concierge's desk, then go through the revolving doors (ahead and to your right as you come off the escalator) to the sidewalk by the Park Avenue viaduct. Turn left on the sidewalk (toward 42nd Street), and follow the sidewalk around to the south side of Grand Central. The sidewalk ends almost across from the Vanderbilt statue. The statue faces south, and is best viewed on a cloudy day, when the shadows are not too harsh.

About the statue

Upright and alert, *Vanderbilt* gazes over his domain: a wealthy, powerful, intelligent man whose presence you can't fail to notice—or couldn't, were he not placed where few pedestrians venture. Rightly proud of having worked his way up from poverty, he wears his usual lavish winter outfit. The double-breasted coat with fur lapels and cuffs makes him an impressive figure. Like the *Columbus* at Columbus Circle, *Vanderbilt's* upright posture suggests confidence, and the extension of one foot slightly over the edge of his pedestal suggests imminent movement. His right hand is tucked into his vest. The motion of his left hand suggests he's in the middle of an action—perhaps giving an order.

Why, you might ask, is the outstretched hand a gesture of action or command here, while the same gesture seemed ineffectual in the Central Park *Columbus*? The answer lies partly in the expression and pose of each figure. The Central Park *Columbus*, old and tired, looks to heaven to solve his problems. *Vanderbilt*, with his stern mouth, direct gaze, and lifted chin, appears authoritative and in control even though he was 75 years old when this statue was made. Given the context of *Vanderbilt's* posture and expression, the gesture of his left hand naturally seems more decisive.

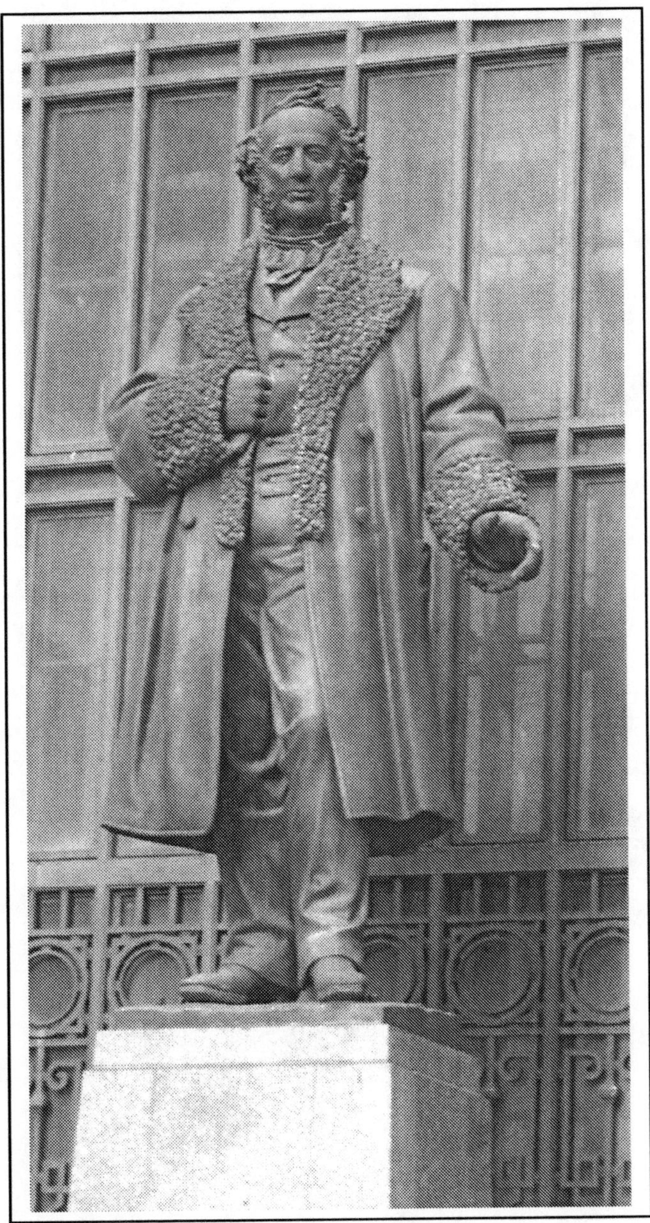

Photo © Dianne L. Durante

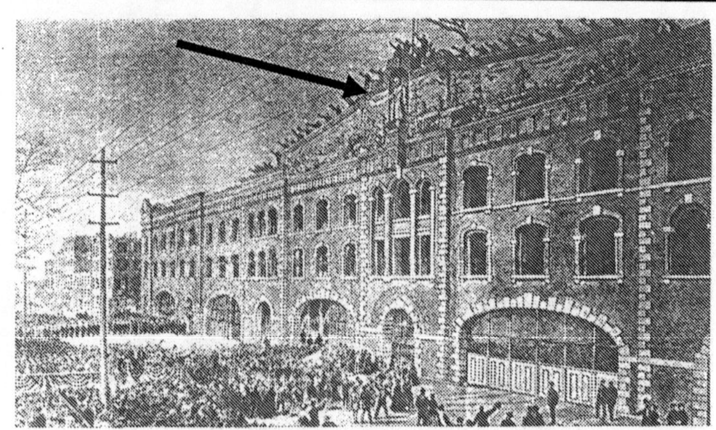

Vanderbilt (center of pediment) and relief at New York Central Railroad terminal in St. John's Park, demolished ca. 1929. Illustration from Lane's *Commodore Vanderbilt.*

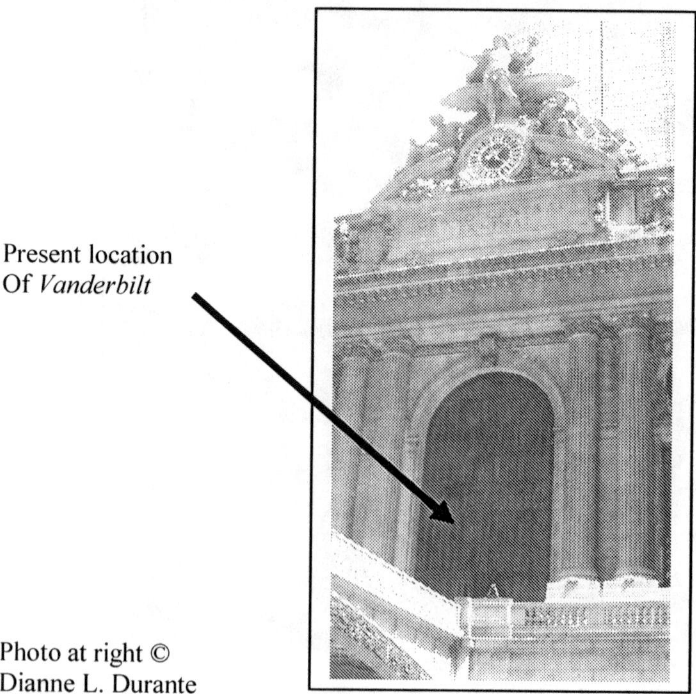

Present location Of *Vanderbilt*

Photo at right © Dianne L. Durante

But there's an even more significant difference between the two gestures. *Vanderbilt's* hand is palm down, *Columbus'* palm upward. Holding one's palm upward always means asking for something. (Think of beggars on subways.) Just from that minor detail, it's evident that *Columbus* is making a request. *Vanderbilt*, with his palm down and finger pointed, is giving an order.

Vanderbilt's Virtues

What he bought he bought to keep, to build up, and to make more productive. ... It required skill, patience, and that mental quality which we call forethought, to conduct successfully such vast concerns as those which employed Vanderbilt's energies. He gave his undivided attention to one branch of business until he saw it was time to leave it. When other men would have followed a line until it began to droop, he resolutely left his in its apparent vigor and seized upon another. In this way the sail-boat was replaced by the steamer, the steamer by a marvel of mechanical skill; the stage-coach gave way to the railway train, and the thin, poorly-equipped railroad line was in turn transformed into the most complete iron highway on the continent. Whatever he did was done well. On all his methods might have been written 'Thorough.' Every movement of his will was perceptible in the fleets which covered the waters, or in the network of rails which enmeshed the land. By him, therefore, the movements of population, the currents of trade and travel, and the requirements of commerce, must have been clearly seen and understood. It was his business, in a large way, to anticipate and meet all these requirements and changes. He did this so well that he is now set down as a highly successful man.

—Vanderbilt's obituary in the *New York Times*, 1/5/1877

The *Vanderbilt* is also an excellent illustration of the importance of setting. In 1869, when it was cast, it was placed at the center of a 150-foot-long, 31-foot-high bronze relief on the facade of Vanderbilt's Hudson River Railroad Freight Depot, just south of Canal Street. The relief showed sailboats, steamboats and railroads: the transportation industries at which Vanderbilt made his millions.

When the Depot was demolished in 1929, the relief was destroyed and Vanderbilt's statue was moved to its present location. There it is dwarfed by the enormous windows of the Terminal, and vanishes against their dark colors. Is the present obscure setting merely due to a lack of foresight? The muckrakers as a recognizable group of writers were gone by 1910 or so, but their attitude toward businessmen was not forgotten. Josephson's *Robber Barons,* which viciously attacked Vanderbilt and other nineteenth-century capitalists and industrialists, was published in 1934. It's certainly possible that in 1929 Cornelius Vanderbilt and his statue were embarrassments to the owners of the railroad.

About the subject

Cornelius Vanderbilt (1794-1877), an uneducated farmer's son, was worth about $100 million when he died—probably the wealthiest man in America. He earned his first million dollars in ships, ferrying passengers by sailboat as a teenager, then switching to steam. So safe and efficient was the service Vanderbilt provided that a series of rivals either sold out to him or paid him to operate elsewhere. By age 45 (1841) he owned or had an interest in more steamboats than anyone else in the country, and had earned the nickname "Commodore."

Meanwhile, after Peter Cooper designed the first American-made steam locomotive in America in 1830, the railroad industry boomed. Small wonder: the trip by rail from Buffalo to Albany took a mere thirty hours, while the trip by the twenty-year-old Erie Canal took ten days. The cost of shipping, and hence the cost of goods, plummeted. Privately financed and privately built railroads spread across the country. Vanderbilt, in his 60s, astonished contemporaries once again by selling out of a prosperous enterprise and applying his formidable energy to the acquisition of railroads. (See sidebar.) By 1857 he was a director of one New York railroad line, and by the early 1860s he owned a controlling interest in the only two railroads that ran into Manhattan.

Why only two? Because in the 1830s, New York politicians decreed who could build lines into Manhattan, how far south steam locomotives could run (at first to Canal, later only to 42nd Street), and whether existing lines could merge. Such political control was often used as a weapon by Vanderbilt's enemies and by speculators who could not match Vanderbilt in offering profit-making services, but who thought they could outmaneuver him in the legislature. After one such abortive attempt, Daniel Drew, Jay Gould and James Fisk, who had attempted to short his stock, had to flee to the wilds of Jersey City to escape prosecution.

On lines he controlled, Vanderbilt improved service and equipment by adding double tracks (for passengers and freight) and upgrading rolling stock and bridges. Horace Greeley, outspoken publisher of the *New York Herald* and a regular commuter on Vanderbilt's Harlem Railroad, commented in 1867 that "We lived on this road when it was poor and feebly managed—with rotten cars and wheezy old engines that could not make schedule time; and the improvement since realized is gratifying. It is understood that the road now pays, and, if so, we are glad of it." (Quoted in Lane, p. 205)

So efficiently did Vanderbilt run his railroads that even in the depression of the 1870s they paid dividends of six to eight percent. Soon he was known as "The Railroad King" as well as "Commodore." Grand Central Depot, completed at 42nd Street in 1871, was one of the largest enclosed spaces in the world. Within a few years, it became too small for its volume of traffic.

Under Vanderbilt's leadership railroads linked New York to Albany in the 1850s and to Chicago by the early 1870s. He lived to see the Credit Mobilier scandal explode after the federal government offered incentives to build a transcontinental railroad, and in 1873 commented on corruption in the railroads with his usual brusque common sense: "These worthless roads prejudice the commercial credit of our country abroad. Building railroads from nowhere to nowhere at public expense is not a legitimate undertaking." (Quoted in Lane, p. 275)

Vanderbilt, often reviled as a "robber baron," was in fact a man who offered high-quality services that the public was eager to buy. As the *New York Times* commented in his obituary, "By him, therefore, the movements of population, the currents of trade and travel, and the requirements of commerce, must have been clearly seen and understood. It was his business, in a large way, to anticipate and meet all these requirements and changes." (See sidebar.)

Bibliography and further reading

Gayle & Cohen p. 122. SIRIS control #IAS 76002815. Stokes 5:1936. For a contemporary comment on the sculpture see George Templeton Strong, *Diary*, ed. Allan Nevins and Milton Halsey Thomas (New York, 1952), vol. 4, pp. 259-60 (entries for Nov. 11 and Nov. 15, 1869). As usual, Strong is snide and condescending: he calls the community of New York "rotten and snobbish enough for almost any conceivable baseness," conjectures that funds for the statue were raised by "jackals and subordinates," and calls the statue itself "bestial."

On Vanderbilt, see Wheaton J. Lane, *Commodore Vanderbilt: An Epic of the Steam Age* (1942), and John F. Stover, "Vanderbilt, Cornelius" (http://www.anb.org/articles/10/10-01678.html; American National Biography Online Feb. 2000, with bibliography). Several obituaries appeared in the *New York Times*, 1/5/1877. On the Vanderbilts and the New York Central Railroad, see Kurt C. Schlichting, *Grand Central Terminal: Railroads, Engineering, and Architecture in New York City* (Baltimore and London, 2001).

For more on railroads in New York, see the essays on Cooper, Holley and Rea in this volume (Numbers 6, 12, 16). For more on Grand Central Terminal, see the essay on *Transportation* in the forthcoming Forgotten Delights volume on allegories. For more on Greeley, see the forthcoming Forgotten Delights volume on politicians and media moguls.

On businessmen as traders by voluntary exchange to mutual benefit, see Ayn Rand, "The Objectivist Ethics," *Virtue of Selfishness* p. 31, and *For the New Intellectual* p. 53.

Etymological tidbit: the term "muckraker" was first used by Theodore Roosevelt in a 1906 speech, in which (paraphrasing Bunyan's *Pilgrim's Progress*) he denounced "the Man with the Muckrake ...who could look no way but downward."

Provenance

The sculpture was the brainchild of Albert DeGroot (1813-1884), a close friend of Vanderbilt and captain of two of Vanderbilt's steamboats. For years the statue was mistakenly attributed to him; on the attribution of the statue to Plassman, see David M. Kahn in *Connoisseur*, June 1980. Dedicated 1869 on the pediment of the Hudson River Railroad Freight Depot near Canal Street. Moved to Grand Central in 1929. Inscription on the present pedestal: "Cornelius Vanderbilt, Founder of the New York Central Railroad." Ownership not stated by Gayle & Cohen or SIRIS: possibly Grand Central or Amtrak.

Essay Number 10

1860

William Earl Dodge

"The Christian Merchant"

Artist: John Quincy Adams Ward

Dedicated: 1885

Medium and size: Bronze (7.5 feet), later granite pedestal (6.5 feet). Richard Morris Hunt's original pedestal has been destroyed.

Location: North side of Bryant Park, just south of 42nd Street and east of Sixth Avenue. The sculpture faces west and is among many trees: best to see it in the afternoon, and if possible when the leaves have fallen.

About the statue

Until now, all the sculptures we've examined stood or sat staunchly, confidently upright. *Dodge*, in contrast, sways elegantly as he rests an elbow on a pile of books atop a column. Nor is it an ancient Doric column like the one that supports *Morse's* telegraph: it's a new-fangled style. A contemporary writer praised the sculpture for capturing Dodge's fine appearance and cordial manner as he delivered a speech. Given Dodge's incessant involvement in committees (see below), that would certainly be an appropriate moment to represent in his portrait statue. Perhaps the scrap of paper he toys with holds notes.

The pose, the dapper outfit, the books, and the style of the column tell us that *Dodge* is not only a wealthy man but an elegant gentleman of learning and culture. The position of his head and the expression on his face confirm this: rather than looking ahead, he tilts his head and gazes meditatively into the distance.

One small but significant detail is missing from this statue. The original base (by noted architect Richard Morris Hunt) had a small drinking fountain, included because Dodge was an ardent advocate of temperance. Nineteenth-century temperance advocates scattered fountains throughout the City so that citizens could have easy access to water rather than liquor.

About the subject

I assigned William Earl Dodge (1805-1883) to *Forgotten Delights: The Producers* because he co-founded Phelps Dodge, still one of the world's foremost copper producers. While Dodge was its leading partner (1834-1860), Phelps Dodge expanded from importing metals to promoting American mining, including Pennsylvania iron and Lake Superior copper. The company produced the copper used on the first transcontinental telegraph line in 1861 and invested heavily in railroads, partly because they helped Phelps Dodge efficiently transport raw materials and finished goods.

But the first draft of *The Producers* contained almost no information about Dodge himself. He's the only individual in this volume who doesn't have an entry in the authoritative and up-to-date *American National Biography*. After a few brief mentions in nineteenth-century biographical dictionaries, Dodge vanished.

Stubbornly, I kept searching for him. I read an adulatory biography by a contemporary. I checked twenty citations in *Gotham: A History of New York City*. I compiled an excruciatingly boring list (which I'll spare you) of the charities and committees to which Dodge donated much of his time and money.

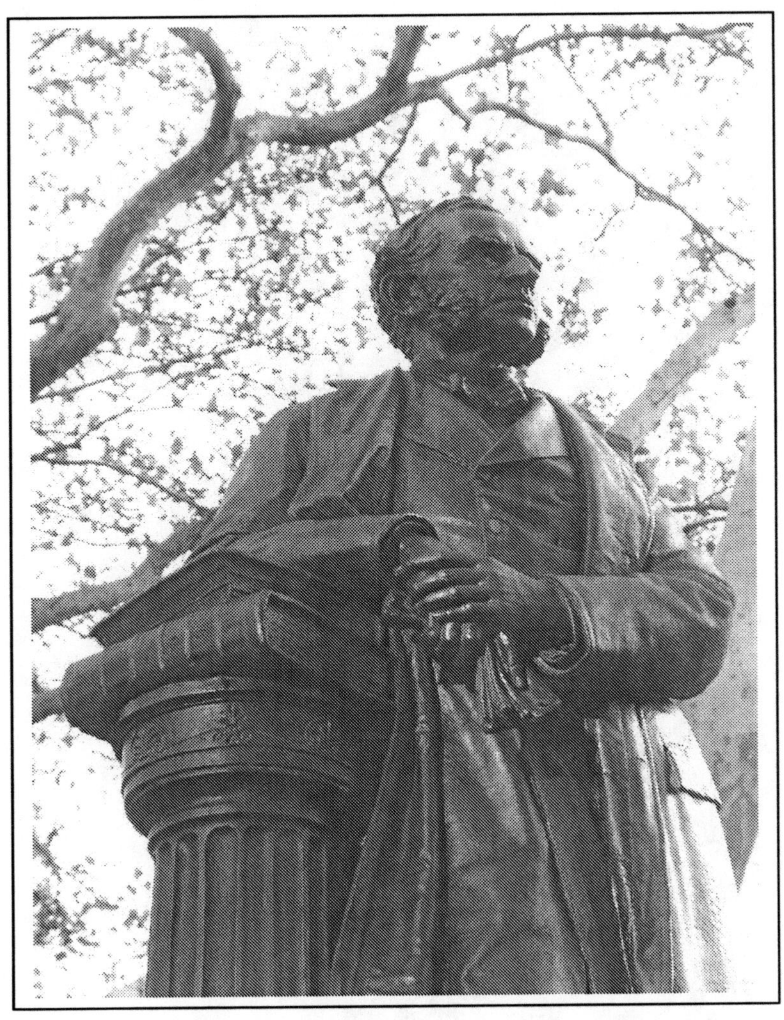

Photo () Dianne L. Durante

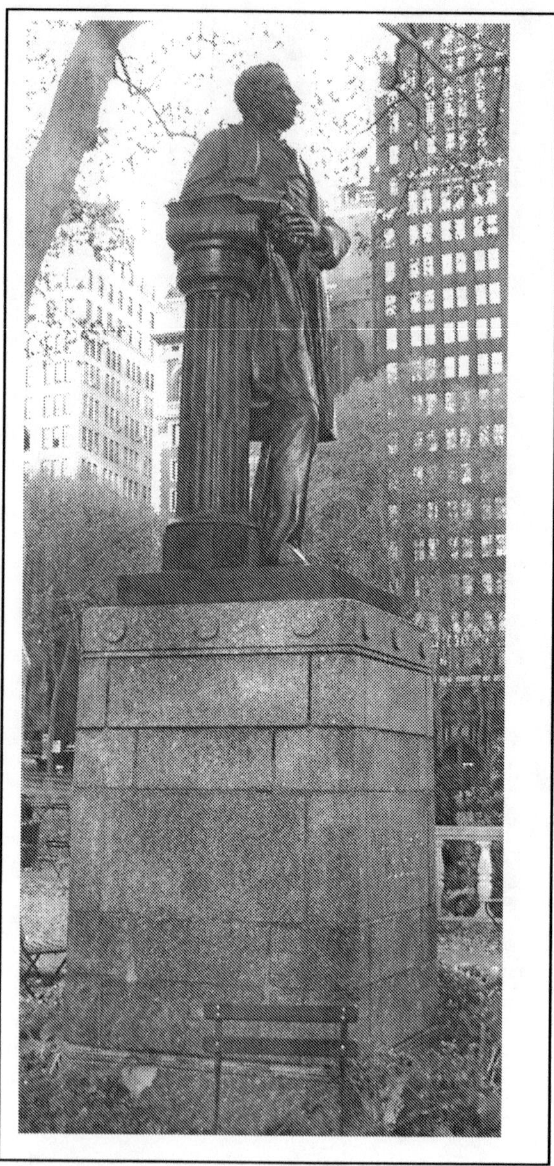

Photo © Dianne L. Durante

But I still couldn't find a single noteworthy productive effort in Dodge's working life on which to center this essay.

Why Honor Dodge?

New-York has not been prodigal of public statues. The erection of such memorials is a privilege which should not be lightly sought, or readily granted. It is the highest honor which can be paid to a citizen, that his memory and features shall be preserved in bronze or marble for the reverent homage of future generations. As a rule, the lapse of time and the favorable judgment of posterity should decide the claim for such eminent recognition. We have not yet erected statues to Fulton, who gave us steam navigation, or to Dewitt Clinton, who created [the Erie Canal,] the highway of commerce which has made New-York great and rich. All men will agree that too much honor cannot be paid to the memory of such public benefactors by the generations which have inherited their glory and profited by their genius....

Even with all his virtues fresh in our minds, and with the fruits of his long and well-spent life in our possession and enjoyment, we cannot venture to compare [Dodge's] unquestionable merits with the achievements of the great men who laid the foundations of our commercial supremacy.

But there are men who can wait for recognition, and there are, on the other hand, characters which demand present recognition, if recognition is ever to be given.

—Abram S. Hewitt, 1886 (*Proceedings of the Unveiling of the Statue of William E. Dodge*, p. 25)

At this point I realized that the problem lay not in my research, but in Dodge himself. Dodge was nicknamed "the Christian Merchant," which implies a contradiction. He ran his business efficiently and with integrity, which requires making judgments based on the facts of reality. Yet as a Christian, he had to have faith in the supernatural, be committed to selfless service to others, and be humble.

How did he reconcile the two? He managed Phelps Dodge, but sat on dozens of charitable committees. He became wealthy, but gave away untold thousands of dollars—often anonymously—to a vast number of causes. Even his colleagues in the Chamber of Commerce, who admired Dodge's efforts and contributed the funds for this statue, recognized that Dodge's widely dispersed efforts would make him far less memorable than men such as Vanderbilt or Cooper. "There are men who can wait for recognition," said Abram Hewitt at the statue's dedication, "and there are, on the other hand, characters which demand present recognition, if recognition is ever to be given." (See sidebar.)

I could have omitted Dodge from this volume: I doubt you would have missed him. But he introduces an interesting point about commemorative sculpture in New York. Although I don't admire Dodge for his focus on charity, his fellow members of the Chamber of Commerce did. They paid for this statue in 1885 so that passersby could remember, admire and emulate Dodge. Indeed, all the sculptures in this volume dedicated in 1910 or earlier share that purpose. Chronologically by date of dedication (rather than by date of achievement), they are *Humboldt, Vanderbilt* and *Morse* (1869-1870), the *Pilgrim* and *Holley* in the 1880s, the two *Columbus* statues, *Sims, Cooper* and *Ericsson* in the 1890s, and *Verrazzano* and *Rea,* in the opening decade of the 1900s.

After that, no more sculptures of specific productive individuals were erected in public view. The later sculptures in this book (all dedicated in the 1970s and 1980s) show anonymous figures who may provoke thought, but do not provide inspiration: *The Immigrants, Double Check, Taxi*, and *The Garment Worker.*

Bibliography and further reading

On the statue and Dodge, see *Proceedings of the Unveiling of the Statue of William E. Dodge, Erected Under the Auspices of the Chamber of Commerce of the State of New-York* (1886), especially Abram Hewitt's speech (pp. 25-32). Gayle & Cohen p. 154. SIRIS control #IAS 76003485.

On Dodge, see W. Carlos Martyn, *William E. Dodge: The Christian Merchant* (1890). See also the lengthy article by Richard Lowitt in *Encyclopedia of American Business History and Biography: Railroads in the Nineteenth Century*, ed. Robert L. Frey (New York and Oxford, 1988), pp. 98-104; *National Cyclopedia of American Biography* III, 174-5; *Dictionary of American Biography* V, 353; and James E. Mooney's entry on Phelps Dodge in *Encyclopedia of New York City* (ed. Kenneth E. Jackson), p. 896. Neither the printed nor the online *American National Biography* has an entry for Dodge. Burrows and Wallace mention Dodge in *Gotham* some twenty times, but only once in relation to his business; see pp. 337, 434, 437-8, 655, 830, 860, 867, 873, 877, 881, 897, 899, 903, 904, 964, 977, 1033, 1082, 1193, 1206.

For more on the railroads, see the essays in this volume on Cooper, Vanderbilt, Holley and Rea (Numbers 6, 9, 12, 16). For more on the telegraph, see Essay Number 7 on Morse.

Provenance

Gift by public subscription of 380 friends and colleagues under the auspices of the Chamber of Commerce of the State of New York. In 1941 *Dodge* was moved it from its original location at Herald Square (Sixth Avenue and 35th Street, with a semi-circular paved area and benches) to its present location, in order to make room for the *J.G. Bennett Memorial* (the *Bellringers' Memorial*; see Forgotten Delights volume on allegories). The original pedestal by Richard Morris Hunt was replaced at that time. Inscription on front of the present base: "William Earl Dodge." Inscription on back of present base: "Erected by voluntary subscription under the auspices of the Chamber of Commerce of the State of New York 1885." Collection of the City of New York.

Essay Number 11

1861

John Ericsson

[T]he object of the Merrimack on the 9th of March was to complete the destruction of the Union fleet in Hampton Roads, and ... in this she was completely foiled and driven off by the *Monitor*. —Greene

Artist: Jonathan Scott Hartley

Dedicated: 1893; second version cast 1902, dedicated 1903.

Medium and size: Bronze (10 feet), on a granite pedestal (11 feet) with four bronze reliefs (each 12 x 27.5 inches).

Location: Battery Park, north end of Eisenhower Mall, between Castle Clinton and Battery Place. The statue faces south, but is situated in a shady area of Battery Park and has a fence that keeps visitors at a distance. Take binoculars.

About the statue

When *Ericsson* was unveiled in 1893, to a 21-gun salute and a lengthy parade, New Yorkers saw a man standing languidly, gesturing with a compass in his right hand to a small square of paper in his left. (See sketch from the *New York Times*, 4/15/1893.) The swaying figure didn't look much like the Ericsson who had for decades been a familiar sight in New York, and whose ironclad battleship the *Monitor* had saved New Yorkers, they believed, from a Confederate naval attack.

The sculptor, Hartley, was so dissatisfied with the original version that he had a revised model cast at his own expense. Rededicated with another 21-gun salute in 1903, *Ericsson* now stands tall and confident, with a stern look to his mouth and a frown on his brow. In one hand is a roll of blueprints, in the other a model of the *Monitor;* the compass has been tidily put away in his pocket. As I noted when describing Morse, a good portrait shows more than physical appearance: it shows a characteristic pose and expression, one that is consistent with the sitter's personality and accomplishments. This second version of *Ericsson* fulfills that requirement. The first did not.

Reliefs on the pedestal display several of Ericsson's inventions. On the front is the *Princeton*, the first screw-propelled vessel of war—still bearing the masts and rigging of a sailing vessel. On *Ericsson's* left the *Monitor* battles the *Merrimac*. Behind him is a rotary gun carriage. To his right, firemen battle a raging blaze using the steam-driven fire engine for which Ericsson won a prize in 1840, an era when flames often destroyed hundreds of New York City buildings at a time.

About the subject

On January 30, 1862, the day of the *Monitor*'s launch, New Yorkers crowded the shores of the East River, expecting a catastrophe. The ship was constructed mostly of iron: how could she possibly move, or even float? Thomas Rowland, one of Ericsson's builders, recalled:

> It was the opinion of most shipbuilders that she would 'throw pitch pole'—that is to say, her stern would go immediately down into the water to run into those tanks just in proportion as the vessel should be immersed in the water while leaving the ways. She was the mud at the bottom of the river and she would turn a somersault.

Photo ©
Dianne L. Durante

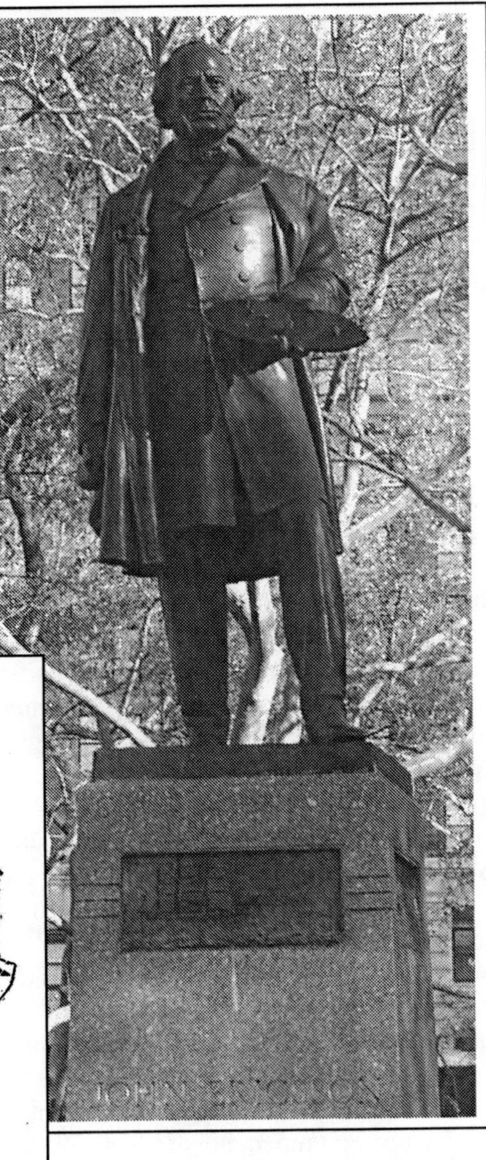

The Statue of Ericsson.

Sketch of original *Ericsson* from *New York Times,* 1893

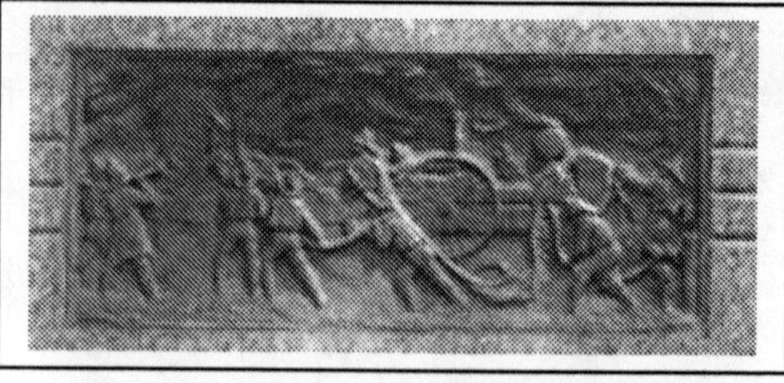

Photo © Dianne L. Durante

> But her peculiarities I had provided for by putting air tanks under her stern and by an automatic device allowing the air to escape and enabled thereby to slide into the water as quietly as a duck going into a pond to swim. Her decks were scarcely wet. Capt. Ericsson stood at the extreme stern and would certainly have been drowned had the fears of those ancient shipbuilders proved correct. (*New York Times* 9/14/1890)

Why was this floating tin can built?

In late 1861, the North learned that a Confederate ironclad would soon be ready to devastate the Union's port cities. The Confederacy had raised the frigate *Merrimac* from Norfolk harbor, christened it the *CSS Virginia* and iron-plated the charred hulk. Confederates boasted of "the immense power and strength of the *Merrimac* in the most extravagant manner" (*New York Times* 3/10/1862). Stiles notes that she was "a jury-rigged vessel with barely functioning engines but still the most powerful warship afloat" (p. 68)—simply because she could withstand shelling indefinitely while mercilessly bombarding her opponents.

The Navy urgently invited proposals for a Union ironclad. Ericsson (1803-1889), a Swedish-born naval engineer with four decades of experience, proposed a radically different type of warship: small and maneuverable, with two powerful guns in a rotating turret, a low, stable design, and propeller and engines tucked below the waterline. After a struggle with the Navy Board (see sidebar), Ericsson was awarded the contract.

"Returning immediately to New York," he wrote,

> I divided the work among three leading mechanical establishments, furnishing each with detailed drawings of every part of the structure; the understanding being that the most skillful men and the best tools should be employed; also that work should be continued

during night-time when practicable. The construction of nearly every part of the battery accordingly commenced simultaneously, all hands working with the utmost diligence, apparently confident that their exertions would result in something of great benefit to the national cause. Fortunately no trouble or delay was met at any point; all progressed satisfactorily; every part sent on board from the workshops fitted exactly the place for which it was intended.

One can only speculate how much of Ericsson's "rude and forcible eloquence" such coordination and speed required, from three independent shops in Brooklyn and Manhattan in the dead of winter. "Capt. Ericsson was a very stern, positive man," said his builder Rowland, "but he was easy enough to get along with if you did what he told you to do. I always did, and so never had any trouble with him."

Ericsson vs. the Bureaucrats

With his previous experience of the waste of time and patience required to accomplish anything at Washington, Captain Ericsson, who is not, it must be said, like the man Moses, 'exceeding meek,' would not himself go to the capital to secure attention to his ideas. [Mr. C.S. Bushnell] went to Washington, but failed in the attempt to persuade the iron-clad board that the designer of the Princeton was worthy of a hearing. Nothing remained except to induce Ericsson to visit Washington in person and plead his own cause with that rude but forcible eloquence which has seldom failed him in an emergency. To move him was only less difficult than to convince the Navy Department without him.

At last a subterfuge was adopted. Ericsson was given to understand that Mr. Bushnell's reception at Washington had been satisfactory and that nothing remained but for him to go on and complete the details of a contract for one of his vessels. Presenting himself before the board, what was his astonishment to find that he was not only an unexpected but apparently an unwelcome visitor! It was evident that the board were asking themselves what could have brought him there. He was not left long in doubt as to the meaning of his reception. To his indignation, as well as his astonishment, he was informed that the plan of a vessel submitted by him had already been rejected.

The first impulse was to withdraw at once. Mastering his anger, however, he stopped to inquire the reason for the determination of the board. The vessel had not sufficient stability, Commodore Smith exclaimed; in fact, it would upset and place her crew in the inconvenient and undesirable position of submarine divers. Now, if there is anything which especially distinguishes the Monitor, *with its low free-board, it is the peculiarity which it has in common with the raft it resembles—its inability to upset. In a most earnest and lucid argument, Captain Ericsson proceeded to explain this. Perceiving that his explanation had its effect, and his blood being well warmed by this time, he ended by declaring to the board with great earnestness: "Gentlemen, after what I have said, I consider it to be your duty to the country to give me an order to build the vessel before I leave this room."*

—Col. William Church in *The Century Magazine*, April 1879
(reprinted in *Battles and Leaders of the Civil War*, I, 750)

In early March, as the *Monitor* wallowed her way south through heavy seas ("The water came down under the turret like a waterfall," noted Executive Officer Dana S. Greene), the telegraph flashed the news to New York and Washington that the *Merrimac*, on her maiden run, had rammed and sunk a 50-gun Union frigate at Hampton Roads, set another on fire, and run a third aground. In a single day's battle, the South suddenly had the chance to break the Union blockade and become an international sea power. In New York there was a "feeling of dread, akin to panic." The Common Council was instructed to appropriate the enormous sum of $500,000 for harbor defenses, "at any sacrifice and at every hazard."

When she arrived at Chesapeake Bay, the *Monitor* was immediately sent on to Hampton Roads. Next day the crew of the *Merrimac*, returning to destroy the grounded Union vessel, spied a strange object nearby: "an immense shingle floating on the water, with a gigantic cheese box rising from its center; no sails, no wheels, no smokestack, no guns" (quoted in Ward, Burns, p. 101). In view of 20,000 cheering Union and Confederate troops, the ships battled for four and a half hours, sometimes close enough to bump hulls, but with negligible damage to either ship. Finally the *Merrimac* lumbered back to harbor to restock her ammunition. That night both sides celebrated victory, although the day's result had been a stalemate.

But long term, the *Monitor's* actions were decisive, as Executive Officer Greene noted: "[T]he object of the *Merrimack* on the 9th of March was to complete the destruction of the Union fleet in Hampton Roads, and...in this she was completely foiled and driven off by the *Monitor*."

The Union blockade remained intact. The *Merrimac* was bottled up harmlessly in Hampton Roads until the Confederates were faced with the loss of Richmond and Norfolk: then they sunk her, since she drew too much water to sail upriver.

Although the *Monitor* was only in service for a few months (she went down in a storm off Cape Hatteras in late 1862), her effect on naval warfare was profound.

> For the previous three hundred years, the fate of nations had been decided by huge, lumbering ships of the line, great clumsy square riggers carrying up to 120 guns and manned by enormous crews of anywhere from five hundred to twelve hundred men. Then, on the morning of March 9, 1862 ... the nimble little *Monitor*, armed with only two eleven-inch Dahlgrens, and manned by a crew of only fifty-eight men, relegated every ship of the line to the scrap heap and established an entirely new set of priorities for the navies of the world. (deKay p. 1)

Shortly after hearing of the battle of the American ironclads, the British Navy—the most formidable in the world—cancelled all outstanding orders for wooden sailing ships. Iron construction, iron plating and turrets were to be the characteristics of the warship of the future. In the United States alone sixty-six *Monitor*-type vessels were built, the last of which remained in service until 1925, sixty-three years after the original *Monitor* was launched.

Bibliography and further reading

On the statue, see *New York Times* 4/15/1893, 8/2/1903. Gayle & Cohen p. 5. SIRIS control #IAS 76003495.

On Ericsson, see Michael A. Cavanaugh. "Ericsson, John"; http://www.anb.org/articles/05/05-00220.html (American National Biography Online Feb. 2000). The account of Ericsson's trip to Washington and his own highly technical account of the *Monitor* appear in *Battles and Leaders of the Civil War*, v. 1 (New York, 1887), pp. 750 and 730-744. See T.J. Stiles, *In Their Own Words: Civil War Commanders*, pp. 67-69 on the importance of the battle between the *Monitor* and the *Merrimac* and pp. 69-75 for the launch of the *Monitor* and an account of the battle of the ironclads by S. Dana Greene, executive officer of the *Monitor*.

For contemporary stories on the *Monitor*, see Rowland's account in *New York Times* 9/14/1890; 3/10/1862 and 3/13/1862 on the battle of the *Monitor* and the *Merrimac*; 3/9/1889 and 3/12/1889 on Ericsson's death and obsequies. A recent, well-written popular account is James Tertius deKay, *Monitor: The Story of the Legendary Civil War Ironclad and the Man Whose Invention Changed the Course of History*, 1997. For photographs, see Geoffrey C. Ward, Ric Burns and Ken Burns, *The Civil War, An Illustrated History*, pp. 98-102.

Note: The *Merrimac* was christened the *Merrimack*, but the "k" seems to have been deep-sixed even before Union troops sunk her in Hampton Roads, just after the South seceded. Most historians refer to her as the *Merrimac* even though the Confederates renamed her the *Virginia*.

The *Monitor* is being raised, piece by piece, by the National Oceanic and Atmospheric Administration, whose log of the underwater excavation can be found at http://oceanexplorer.noaa.gov/explorations/monitor01/tour/tour.html.

On the devastating fires in early New York that Ericsson's fire engine helped control, see Essay Number 6 on *Cooper* and the essay on the *Bethesda Fountain* in the forthcoming Forgotten Delights volume on allegories.

Provenance

Inscription on base: "The City of New York erects this statue to the memory of a citizen whose genius has contributed to the greatness of the Republic and the progress of the world." Paid for by New York City taxes. Collection of the City of New York.

Essay Number 12

1865

Alexander Lyman Holley

"The Father of Modern American Steel Manufacturing"

Artist: John Quincy Adams Ward

Dedicated: 1890

Medium and size: Bronze bust, over life-size, on a limestone pedestal by Thomas Hastings.

Location: Washington Square, west of the central fountain. Faces west; should be viewed in the afternoon, when the sun is on the face.

About the statue

A million balls of melted iron tearing away from the liquid mass, surging from side to side and plunging down again, only to be blown out more hot and angry than before. Column upon column of air, squeezed solid like rods of glass by the power of 500 horses, piercing and shattering the iron at every point, chasing it up and

> down, robbing it of its treasures, only to be itself decomposed and hurled out into the night in a roaring blaze. As the combustion progresses the surging mass grows hotter, throwing its flashes of liquid slag. And the discharge from its mouth changes from sparks and streaks of red and yellow gas to thick full white dazzling flame. But such battles cannot last long. In a quarter of an hour the iron is stripped of every combustible alloy and hangs out the white flag. The converter is then turned upon its side, the blast shut off, and the carburizer run in. Then for a moment the war of the elements rages again—the mass boils and flames with higher intensity and with a rapidity of chemical reaction, sometimes throwing it violently out of the converter's mouth. Then all is quiet, and the product is steel, liquid, milky steel that pours out into the ladle from under its roof of slag, smooth, shiny, and almost transparent. (Holley, quoted in Morison)

With his direct gaze and upright carriage, Holley appears to be intelligent and levelheaded—desirable characteristics in a man who routinely built and operated the plants for the steel-making process that he described above. His curly hair and the nubbly texture of his overcoat nicely set off his handsome, strong-featured, unlined face with its broad forehead and cavalry mustache. At the right, a twig of oak leaves refers to the honor being paid to him.

Doubtless Holley slept, laughed at jokes and tied his shoes, but this bust presents a stripped-down Holley: the features and expression that show him as the type of man who understood dangerous procedures and complex machinery, and confidently relied on his own judgment to control them. Those characteristics, and of course his detailed knowledge of the Bessemer process (see below), made him invaluable to the American steel industry in the late nineteenth century.

The *New York Times* derided the idea of setting Holley's bust up in a public place: “The time is coming... when sites for statues in the Park will be too scarce to be assigned to effigies from which the general public will derive its first knowledge that the originals of them have existed” (4/24/1890). But like those who donated funds for *Morse, Sims* and *Dodge*, Holley’s colleagues thought he deserved to be honored:

Our heroes are not alone those who have repelled invasion, suppressed rebellion, or broadened our boundaries by conquests of the sword or pen, but in a better sense those who have made the great forces of nature subservient to our purposes, and placed at the command of industry and enterprise the means which have rendered possible a national development that commands the admiration of the world. (James C. Bayles at the dedication of the Holley bust, *New York Times* 10/3/1890)

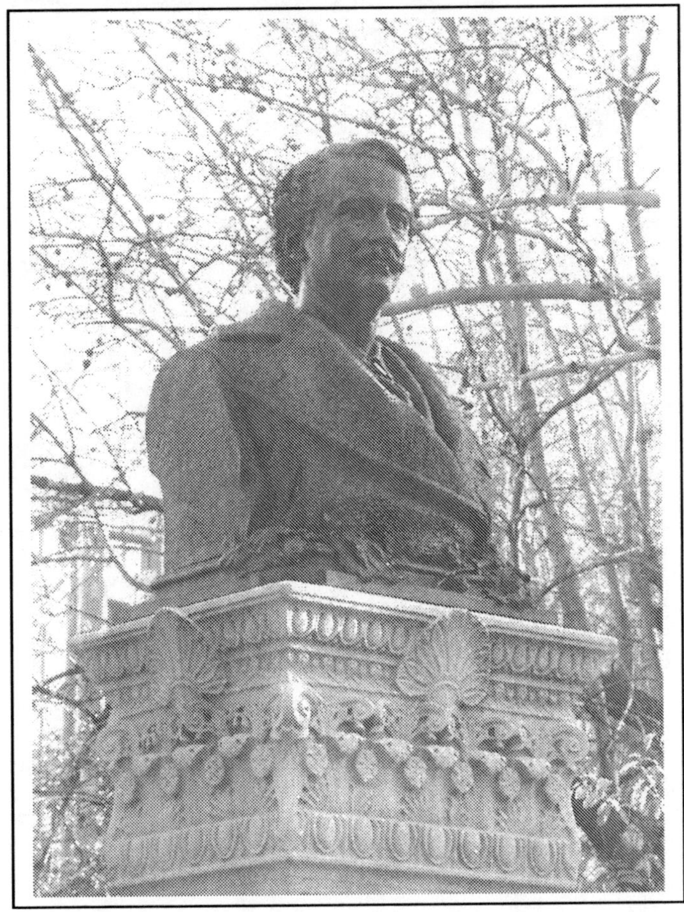

Photo © Dianne L. Durante

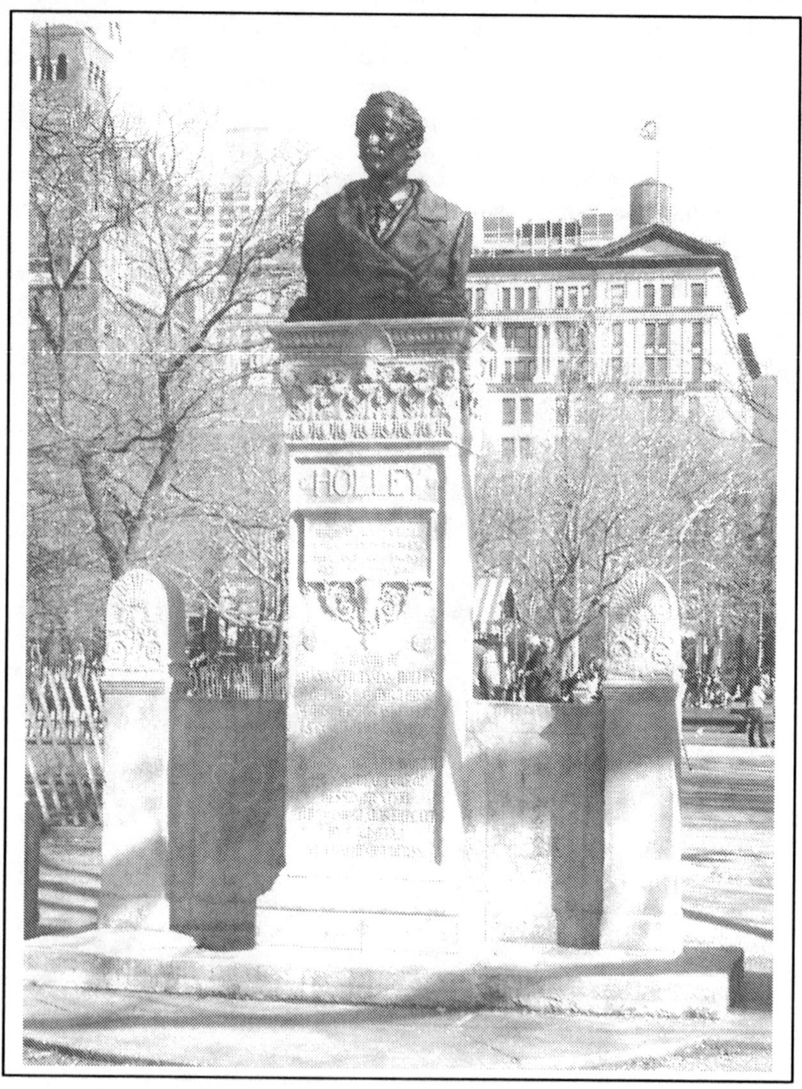

Photo © Dianne L. Durante

About the subject

After the B&O Railroad's success in 1830 (see Essay Number 6 on *Cooper*), railroad tracks snaked rapidly across the United States. A thousand miles were laid by 1835, thirty thousand by 1860. But under the stress of heavy locomotives and freight, iron rails often lasted barely two years. When the next great age of railroad expansion occurred, just after the Civil War, the life of rails was closer to fifteen years, because they were made largely of Bessemer steel—a material whose use in America was brought about almost single-handedly by Alexander Lyman Holley (1832-1882).

Sent to Europe during the Civil War to gather information for the Union about modern weaponry, Holley produced an 1865 landmark work on artillery and gun manufacture. More importantly, on a side trip to Sheffield, England, Holley observed Henry Bessemer's new process for making steel. Steel was more resilient than iron—it lasted five or six times as long—and could be poured or rolled directly into any desired shape. The major advantage of Bessemer's process, however, was its speed.

Before Bessemer's process, steel was only produced in small quantities. To iron extracted from iron ore, a small amount of carbon was added back by layering iron bars with charcoal and heating the two together for days on end. Often the resulting "blister steel" was melted down in order to mix the elements more evenly, and then the whole process was repeated to add more carbon. Producing a small amount of steel might take six weeks. Because of its lack of homogeneity, however, such steel was not much better than wrought iron—although its production was much more time-consuming and labor-intensive.

Bessemer perfected a method of blowing a tremendous blast of air through melted pig iron to remove all impurities, and then adding back the desired amount of carbon while the metal was still molten. (For Holley's description of the process, see "About the statue" above.) A Bessemer converter produced two tons or more of steel in about twenty minutes, and because it was homogeneous and its carbon content precisely controlled, it was higher-grade steel than any produced previously.

Holley immediately grasped that Bessemer's process could have a tremendous impact on American industry. He persuaded his employer to purchase the American rights to the process and to license its use to other American manufacturers.

The New York Times _Celebrates the Grandeur of Modern Metallurgy_

It is neither magic nor alchemy, but straightforward, inductive reasoning and downright, patient, organized, costly work that lays open the great unknown, and utilizes its treasures.

The modern revolution in metallurgy is, perhaps, less striking, but more wonderful than all the others. The wonder of ocean telegraphy is new every morning, while the furnace smokes silently and unobserved. But the smoke of the furnace will tell you tales of nature's secrets unlocked, of startling transformation, of fathomless search, of baffling experiment, of patient endeavor, of endless obstacles, of intellects gone mad, or money burned up, of a forlorn hope fighting against the Powers of the Air, but fighting to win.

Of all the agencies in the material progress of the times, iron, in its various forms and combinations, holds the first place. Its loss would be a calamity only surpassed by the loss of bread; while its cheaper, wide and better production would electrify every human enterprise.

We have thus briefly referred to the grandeur and the difficulty of the great material problem of the age, not to account for failure, but to celebrate success.

—"The Production of Cheap Steel in America. Completion of the Parent Works at Troy," *New York Times* 8/9/1868

Holley's designs were the basis for eleven of the twelve Bessemer plants eventually built in the United States. Beginning in 1865 he supervised construction of most of them, starting with one in Troy, New York, whose technology was celebrated in the *New York Times* (see sidebar). At Andrew Carnegie's massive Edgar Thompson Steel Works in Pittsburgh, built from the ground up, Holley was able most fully to implement his conviction that whenever possible, all the steps from transforming the raw material into the finished product should be performed on one site—a concept fundamental to later American factories.

In just thirteen years production of Bessemer steel rose from 3,000 tons to well over a million. Most of it was used by the railroads. Railroad mileage increased from 39,276 in 1867 to more than 70,000 six years later. The burgeoning railroads not only transformed American transportation, but dominated American business and the stock market, establishing methods of corporate financing and administration that remained the norm for decades.

Five years after the first Bessemer plant opened, thirty-eight-year-old Holley wrote, "I have not got along far enough in life to look back on much work or much fruit from it; but I have lived long enough to conclude with certainty, that leisure is the hardest thing in life to get along with. I try to have as little of it as possible." (Black p. 168) He succeeded admirably. Holley single-handedly kept the owners of Bessemer plants up-to-date on new techniques, both his own (he was granted over a dozen patents for improvements) and those discovered in Europe. He published hundreds of articles and lectured widely to engineers. One of those praised him as "the Moses who led us out of the bondage of cant and custom which made the engineer a worker only and not a thinker as well" (Morison p. 160). It was such grateful colleagues who raised funds for the *Holley* bust in Washington Square.

The last American Bessemer plant was phased out in the 1970s. A hundred years earlier, however, Holley had already recognized the advantages of the Siemens brothers' new open-hearth process of steel making. He convinced several clients of its value but died in 1882, at age 50, before he could supervise construction of such plants.

Holley is a perfect example of the businessman acting as the link between the scientist's theoretical discoveries and the material goods such discoveries make possible. Although not a technological or financial genius, Holley made a respectable living by spreading a new technology. In so doing, he brought radical and beneficial innovations not just to steel makers but to all

American industry. The life of everyone who rode a train or used goods transported by rail—and that meant nearly all Americans—was immeasurably improved by Holley's dedication to doing his best in his chosen field.

Bibliography and further reading

Gayle & Cohen p. 73. SIRIS control #IAS 76003509.

On Holley, see Allida Black, "Alexander Lyman Holley," in *Encyclopedia of American Business History and Biography: Iron and Steel in the Nineteenth Century*, ed. Paul F. Paskoff (New York and Oxford, 1989), pp. 161-72, with substantial technical information; and Stephen H. Cutliffe, "Holley, Alexander Lyman" (http://www.anb.org/articles/13/13-00778.html; American National Biography Online Feb. 2000), with further bibliography.

For an excellent discussion of the development of the steel industry in the United States, which includes the long passage by Holley quoted under "About the Statue," see Elting E. Morison, *Men, Machines and Modern Times* (Cambridge, 1966), Ch. 7: "Almost the Greatest Invention," pp. 122-205. See also the extensive articles in the *New York Times* on Bessemer steel and steel plants in America: 4/4/1860, 7/27/1868, 9/16/1870, 9/27/1870, 10/15/1870.

For more on the early history of railroads, see the essays in this volume on Cooper, Vanderbilt and Rea (Numbers 6, 9, 16), and Thomas Curtis Clarke et al., *The American Railway: Its Construction, Development, Management and Appliances* (ca. 1889; reprinted 1988).

On the businessman as a link between the scientist and consumer, see the title essay in Ayn Rand, *For the New Intellectual* (pb), p. 27.

Provenance

Holley founded or co-founded several professional engineering societies: the American Society of Mechanical Engineers (ASME); the Institute of Mining, Metallurgical and Petroleum Engineers (AIME); and the American Society of Civil Engineers (ASCE). Members of these societies collaborated to raise funds for this monument, whose inscription (now mostly effaced from the soft marble) reads: "In honor of Alexander Lyman Holley, foremost among those whose genius and energy established in America and improved throughout the world the manufacture of Bessemer steel, this memorial is erected by Engineers of Two Hemispheres." On the back of the pedestal are the dates of Holley's birth and death. Collection of the City of New York.

Essay Number13

1884

Marteleur (Metalsmith)

The most ambitious of us try tirelessly to increase the results we can achieve in a given number of hours. —Hazlitt

Artist: Constantin-Emile Meunier

Dedicated: 1914 (sculpted 1884, first exhibited 1886)

Medium and size: Bronze (6.6 feet), on a granite pedestal (3.25 feet) by McKim, Mead and White.

Location: Columbia University, at the entrance to the Engineering Building (northeast corner of the campus, near Amsterdam Avenue and 120th Street). The statue faces south and stands in the open, making it easy to see at any time of day.

About the statue

The *Marteleur*—an anonymous man of average size—heralds a new trend in sculpture. Over the hundred years that follow his creation, sculptures shrink from over-life-size to barely life-size, and subjects shift from captains of industry to workers, from military leaders to foot soldiers, from the famous to the anonymous. In a moment, we'll consider why this happens. First, let's look at the *Marteleur* in detail.

The man represented here is young—his face is unlined. He has wiry strength, not the physique of a body-builder. Judging from his outfit, he works with hot metal: the leather apron, shoe covers and hat all protect him from sparks, while the loose, open-necked shirt helps him stay cool in brutal heat. Although he stands at ease, the large tool in his right hand shows that he has been performing strenuous physical labor. The slight droop of his shoulders suggests fatigue, but the left arm held akimbo, the lifted chin and the gaze fixed in the distance imply that he still has some energy to spare.

When Meunier's works were first exhibited in New York, they were hailed as "the epic of modern industrialism" (*New York Times* 1/17/1914). Is the *Marteleur* meant to represent a new type of epic hero, or to remind us of the plight of the downtrodden, exploited worker? What aspect of this laborer was most important to Meunier? What does Meunier emphasize and what is his attitude toward it?

The *Marteleur* shows a man who has been performing strenuous, fatiguing manual labor. Although Meunier's figures all work, they never display any sense of energy, accomplishment or joy. They are somber figures, like those in Millet's paintings of the 1850s. A *New York Times* critic captured the mood:

> [T]he expression on the faces is solemn and determined, with the sullenness of those who have put their shoulder to the wheel and know that they must keep it indefinitely rolling on without hope of respite or release. (8/17/1913)

The other significant feature of this sculpture is the worker's job. He's an anonymous cog in a manufacturing process, one of many low-level workers needed to mass-produce iron or steel. Meunier's title, *Marteleur,* means simply "The Hammerer." Only a specialist could determine his role in the process.

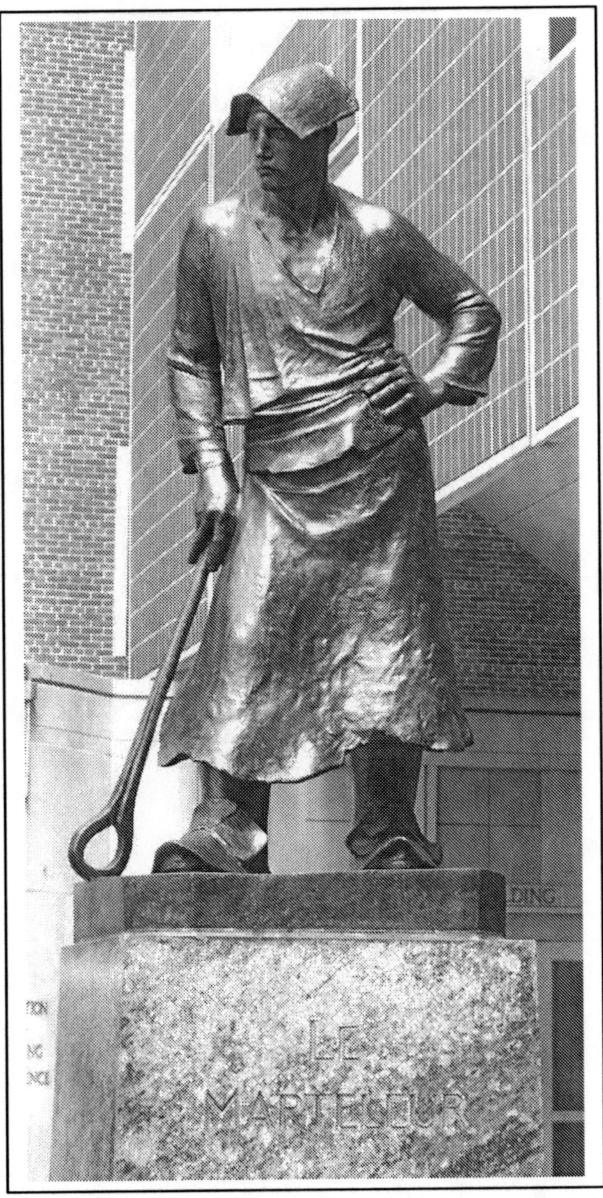

Photo © Dianne L. Durante

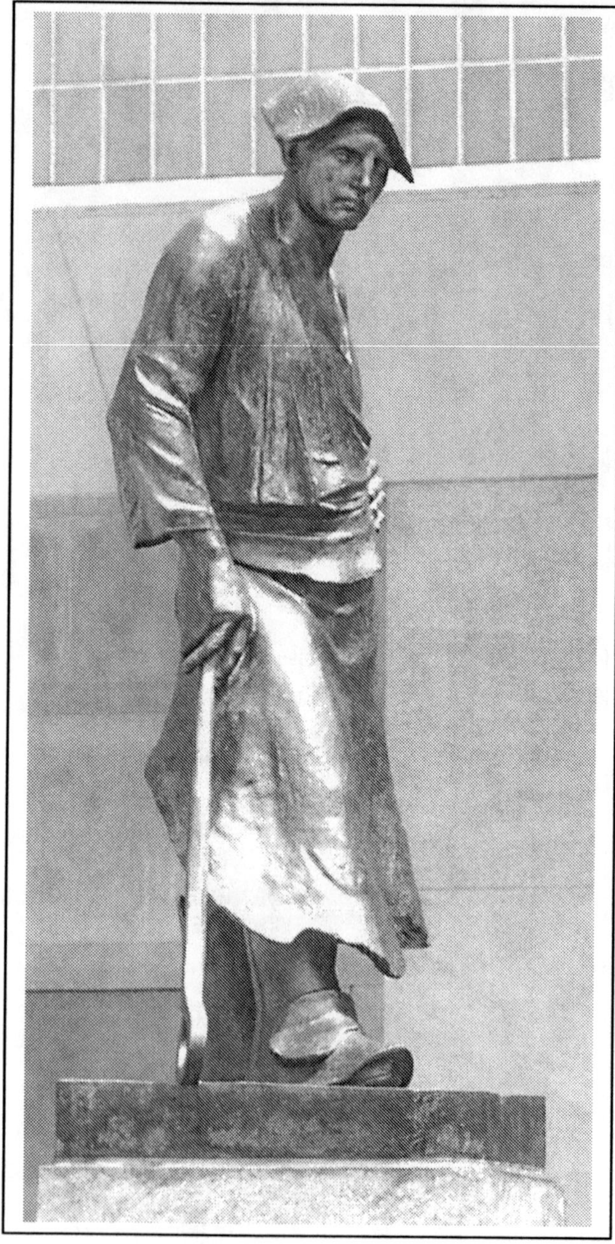

Photo © Dianne L. Durante

Had Meunier been intent on glorifying modern industry, he could have shown a metalworker who had benefited from technology and was proud of what he could accomplish. Instead Meunier represented a lowly worker, fatigued by difficult work in dangerous, sweltering conditions.

A subtle point about this sculpture reveals more about Meunier's attitude toward industry. In literature or film, a few words can call to mind a character, an incident, a whole situation. Narrow your eyes and drawl, "Go ahead, make my day," and you summon the image of Dirty Harry, a cop who broke all the rules but always put the crooks out of action. Compare a colleague to Howard Roark and you evoke the intransigent independence and far-sighted determination of the *Fountainhead*'s hero.

Visual artists achieve the same result by "quoting" the pose or expression of famous works of art. Meunier, who had three years of art education in the mid-nineteenth century (when learning art history was as important as learning the latest in technique), has here "quoted" a well-known bronze sculpture by one of the Renaissance's leading sculptors, Donatello.

Donatello's bronze *David* holds a sword with his right hand; the *Marteleur* holds a long, narrow metalworker's tool. *David's* left arm is akimbo, giving him an air of energy; so is the *Marteleur's*. Donatello's *David* is young (absurdly so, if one is accustomed to Michelangelo's *David*; less so, if one reads the Biblical account), and wears an odd hat. The *Marteleur* is a few years older but still youthful, and wears equally strange headgear.

What does Meunier gain by "quoting" the *David*? He associates all the characteristics of the Biblical David with his *Marteleur*. He makes his anonymous worker a hero. He portrays him as weak but righteous. He pits him against a giant who relies on brute force, thus turning modern industrialists into villains. Because of his resemblance to Donatello's *David,* the *Marteleur* is not a nameless, exhausted cog in a factory, but an underdog who will eventually emerge victorious against a stronger but immoral enemy. With the bend of an arm and the slant of a tool, Meunier has turned a sculpture into political propaganda.

About the subject

Ironically but not coincidentally, it is the *Marteleur* rather than *Holley* who stands on the campus of Columbia University, and not only on the campus but directly outside the Engineering Building. What does he represent? Why is he there? Who paid for him?

The author of an early exhibition catalogue of Meunier's work laments,

> The whole face of the land has been seared and the sky blackened by fumes from countless belching stacks and blast furnaces. Man, in place of remaining bucolic and pastoral, has become a dusky, subterranean creature. His back is bowed and the song upon his lips has turned to a bitter cry for easier hours and better pay. (Brinton p. 34).

As Hazlitt points out (see sidebar), machines are not the cause of "constantly mounting unemployment and misery." In the long run the Bessemer process and other technological achievements improved life immeasurably for men such as this metalworker. He was able to produce quantities of goods and earn wages that would have been inconceivable to his father or grandfather.

Technophobes and Technophiles

If it were indeed true that the introduction of labor-saving machinery is a cause of constantly mounting unemployment and misery, the logical conclusions to be drawn would be revolutionary, not only in the technical field but for our whole concept of civilization. Not only should we have to regard all further technical progress as a calamity; we should have to regard all past technical progress with equal horror. Every day each of us in his own activity is engaged in trying to reduce the effort it requires to accomplish a given result. Each of us is trying to save his own labor, to economize the means required to achieve his ends. Every employer, small as well as large, seeks constantly to gain his results more economically and efficiently—that is, by saving labor. Every intelligent workman tries to cut down the effort nec-

essary to accomplish his assigned job. The most ambitious of us try tirelessly to increase the results we can achieve in a given number of hours. The technophobes, if they were logical and consistent, would have to dismiss all this progress and ingenuity as not only useless but vicious. Why should freight be carried from Chicago to New York by railroad when we could employ enormously more men, for example, to carry it all on their backs?

—Henry Hazlitt, *Economics in One Lesson* (New York, 1979), p. 54

But by the late nineteenth century, even as the Industrial Revolution flourished, a philosophical reaction against it was under way. Intellectuals disparaged the Machine Age and the "exploiters" who ran factories. Absorbing this idea from the intellectuals, painters such as Courbet and Millet glorified peasants whose primitive tools might have come from the Middle Ages rather than the nineteenth century. Industrialists and businessmen became unpopular as subjects. The day of the common, anonymous worker had arrived.

Whatever one thinks of William Earl Dodge's decision to focus on giving wealth away rather than producing it, his statue was erected by colleagues who admired him and thought him worthy of emulation. But this anonymous figure of a manual laborer is not meant to inspire imitation by the highly educated students of the major university on whose campus it stands. It is meant to evoke pity for the worker and disgust for those who employ him.

In the late nineteenth century, the wealth generated by the Industrial Revolution paid for the education of thousands of American students in European universities. They returned home imbued with a distaste or outright hatred for the Industrial Revolution and the capitalism and individualism upon which the Revolution was based. The *Marteleur*, donated in 1914 to Columbia University by the Class of 1889, is a conspicuous example of European influence on American culture.

A side note: when I first saw the *Marteleur* I liked his jauntiness, his youth, and the fact that he works for a living. I still like those aspects of the figure, but now that I've learned more about his historical context, I factor that into my opinion of the statue, and respond to him less positively. Further discussion of emotional responses to sculpture will appear in future volumes of Forgotten Delights.

Bibliography and further reading

Gayle & Cohen p. 302. SIRIS control #IAS 87870202.

For an early discussion of Meunier's work, see Christian Brinton, "Official Exhibition Catalogue: Constantin Meunier," produced for the exhibition at Columbia University, Avery Library, 1/27-2/15/1914 (New York, 1914). Substantial articles on Meunier appeared in the *New York Times* 8/17/1913, 11/9/1913 and 2/1/1914.

On the changing intellectual and philosophical trends in late 19th-century Europe and their effects on the education of American youth, see Leonard Peikoff, *The Ominous Parallels*, especially Chapters 6 and 14, and Eric Daniels, "The History of American Moral Thinking" (audiotape available from the Ayn Rand Bookstore).

Provenance

Inscription on base: "Marteleur." Sculpted in 1884. Exhibited in Paris 1886. Purchased for Columbia University by the Class of 1889, from an exhibition of Meunier's work held at Columbia in 1914. Presented at the 1914 commencement. Collection of Columbia University.

Essay Number 14

1900

The Immigrants

Make [the United States] the home of the skilful, the industrious, the fortunate, the happy, as well as the asylum of the distressed ... —Henry

Artist: Luis Sanguino

Dedicated: 1983 (designed 1973)

Medium and size: Bronze, eight life-size figures (10 x 14 feet, 5 feet high), granite base (13 x 17.5 feet, 8 inches high).

Location: Battery Park, just north of Castle Clinton and southeast of the *Ericsson* statue. The kneeling figure at the front faces roughly north. The sides are in deep shadow early and late in the day.

About the statue

Five-week-old macaroni and cheese has a more appealing texture than this sculpture. In *The Immigrants* no distinction is visible between flesh and cloth, hair and luggage. What happened in the century between the *Ericsson* and *The Immigrants* to make this sort of texture not only acceptable, but prevalent?

Blame Auguste Rodin, the late-nineteenth-century French sculptor who popularized rough textures in works such as *The Thinker*. Rodin proclaimed that sculptures ought to appear unfinished. The roughness of the forms and the lack of polish, said he, allow the viewer to "see" the process by which the sculpture is made. For Rodin, having a viewer understand how a sculpture was created was more important than any message the finished work might convey.

But is it indeed more important to see the process than the result—to see the method rather than the content?

If I want to know how sculpture is made, I can sign up for a hands-on class on sculptural technique. A work of art's purpose is not to illustrate method or technique. It is to give a sharp, focused view of what matters in the world. It is a way for an artist to say, "Stop, look, think! This—this thing right here—is really important."

I have stressed throughout this volume that an artist must be selective in making a statue, in his choice of pose, expression, gesture and a thousand other details. This is the goal of the sculptor's selectivity: to present, in a single visual image, a message that the artist considers important.

With respect to surface texture, it's true that an artist's ability to render exquisite detail does not guarantee that he has anything worthwhile to say. He may have disciplined himself to reproduce minute nuances of form and texture, yet have no message to express. In the same way, a computer programmer might memorize every element of HTML code but have no meaningful idea to convey on a website.

But it's also true that lack of detail—or a deliberate suppression of detail, such as we see on *The Immigrants*—makes the message of the sculpture more difficult to decipher. Why? Because it gives us, as viewers, less information to work with, and makes us less inclined to study the work closely.

Consider this particular sculpture. These immigrants are a cultural cross-section of the world's poor: ragged, underfed, surrounded by bags and boxes holding their meager possessions. As

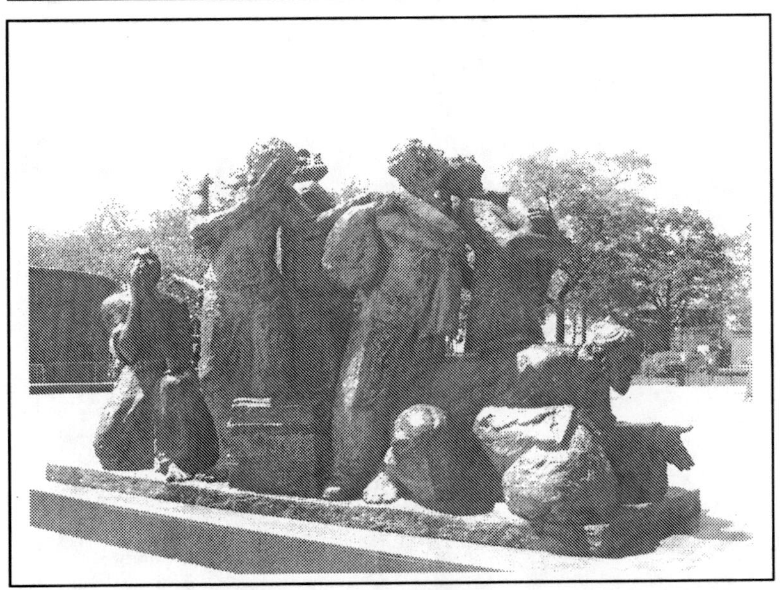

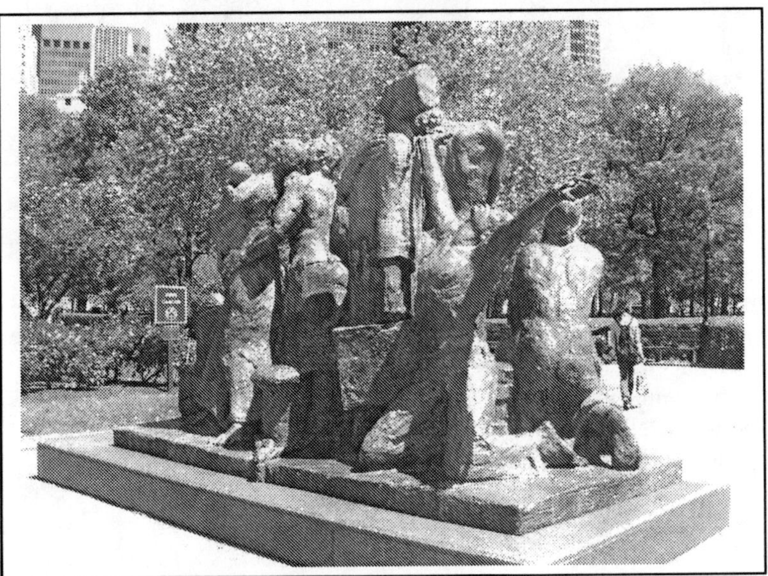

Art © Luis Sanguino. NOTE: If you know how to contact this artist, please email comments@forgottenDelights.com. Photos © Dianne L. Durante.

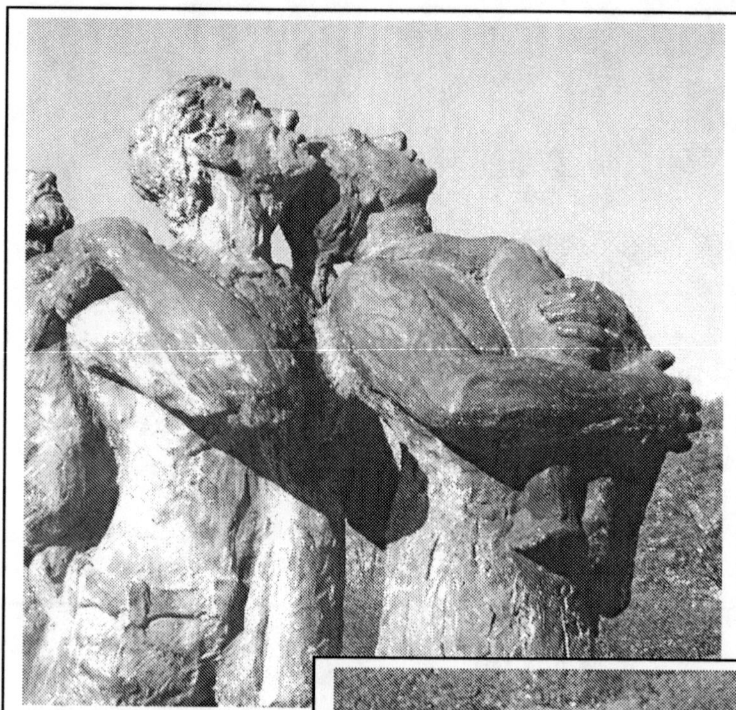

Art © Luis Sanguino.
NOTE: If you know how to contact this artist, please email comments@forgottenDelights.com.
Photos © Dianne L. Durante

they disembark, they raise their faces and their arms heavenward. At the front of the group, a man in a skullcap kneels to touch the land. Through broad gestures and poses, *The Immigrants* conveys the relief of all these people on reaching America. Unfortunately, the thoroughly repulsive texture means we aren't drawn in by the variations in appearance—especially of facial expressions—that might have made us linger to look at the sculpture more closely and ponder what these people are feeling, and why.

About the subject

From Northern, Southern and Eastern Europe, from Asia and Africa, immigrants streamed into the port of New York: thirty-three million between 1815 and 1915. Many stayed in New York, so that by 1910, immigrants made up about 40% of the city's population.

Why did so many use their life savings or borrowed money to travel for months on a stinking, crowded ship, arriving penniless in a country where even the language was unfamiliar? You might answer by focusing on the negative or the positive: why people emigrated from their native lands, or why they immigrated to the United States in particular.

The figures in *The Immigrants* epitomize the negative reasons. They look like an illustration of Emma Lazarus' "The New Colossus," a poem added to the base of the *Statue of Liberty* in 1903 (nineteen years after its dedication):

> "Keep, ancient lands, your storied pomp!" cries she
> With silent lips. "Give me your tired, your poor,
> Your huddled masses yearning to breathe free,
> The wretched refuse of your teeming shore.
> Send these, the homeless, tempest-tost to me.
> I lift my lamp beside the golden door!"

On the positive side, Patrick Henry, in his brilliant 1783 speech (see sidebar), argued that we should welcome "the skilful, the industrious, the fortunate, the happy"—those who, whatever the country of their birth, would improve their own lives by productive effort and, in the course of doing so, increase the prosperity of the United States. Such productive men, Henry argued, would be attracted by America's unprecedented political freedom: "They see a land in which liberty hath taken up her abode—that liberty, whom they had considered as a fabled goddess existing only in the fancies of poets."

Patrick Henry on Immigration

People, sir, form the strength and constitute the wealth of a nation. I want to see our vast forest filled up by some process a little more speedy than the ordinary course of nature. I wish to see these states rapidly ascending to the rank which their natural advantages authorize them to hold among the nations of the earth. ... [E]ncourage emigration—encourage the husbandmen, the mechanics, the merchants of the old world, to come and settle in this land of promise—make it the home of the skilful, the industrious, the fortunate, the happy, as well as the asylum of the distressed—fill up the measure of your population as speedily as you can, by the means which heaven has placed in your hands—and I venture to prophesy there are those now living who will see this favored land among the most powerful on earth—able, sir, to take care of herself ...

Open your doors, sir, and they will come in—the population of the old world is full to overflowing—that population is ground, too, by the oppressions of the governments under which they live. Sir, they are already standing on tiptoe upon their native shores, and looking to your coasts with a wistful and longing eye—they see here a land blessed with natural and political advantages which are not equaled by those of any other country upon earth—a land on which Providence hath emptied the horn of abundance—a land over which peace hath now stretched forth her white wings, and where content and plenty lie down at every door! Sir, they see something more attractive than all this—they see a land in which liberty hath taken up her abode—that liberty, whom they had considered as a fabled goddess existing only in the fancies of poets ... Sir, let but this, our celestial goddess, Liberty, stretch forth her fair hand toward the people of the old world—tell them to come, and bid them welcome—and you will see them pouring in from the north, from

> *the south, from the east, and from the west—your wildernesses will be cleared and settled—your deserts will smile—your ranks will be filled, and you will soon be in a condition to defy the powers of any adversary.*
>
> —Patrick Henry, speech on immigration to the Virginia House of Delegates, 1783 (quoted in William Wirt Henry, *Patrick Henry, Life, Correspondence and Speeches* [1969 reprint] II, 193-5)

To honor the sort of productive immigrants that Patrick Henry had in mind, we must look to other monuments, notably to the *Ericsson*. Ericsson came from Sweden by way of England and settled in the United States, where his engineering innovations conferred an immeasurable benefit on all Americans.

Bibliography and further reading

Gayle & Cohen p. 6. SIRIS control #IAS 87870001.

On immigration and New York, see Burrows and Wallace, *Gotham*, Parts 4 and 5, and Carol Groneman and David M. Reimers, "Immigration," *Encyclopedia of New York City* pp. 581-87 (with useful tables).

For more on art, including Ayn Rand's definition of it as "a selective re-creation of reality according to an artist's metaphysical value-judgments" (the definition on which my comments in "About the Statue" are based), see *The Romantic Manifesto* (New York, 1975), especially Chapters 1-4.

Copies of Rodin's *Thinker* are on display at the Metropolitan Museum of Art and on the Columbia University campus, near the *Marteleur*. On the *Thinker* and the *Statue of Liberty*, see the forthcoming Forgotten Delights volume on allegories.

Provenance

The inscription on the base of the statue reads, "The Immigrants. Dedicated to the people of all nations who entered America through Castle Garden, in memory of Samuel Rudin, 1896-1975, whose parents arrived in America in 1888." Gift of Samuel and May Rudin. Collection of the City of New York.

Essay Number 15

1901

The Garment Worker

We are crawling up, yea, bursting up ... There is no power on earth that can permanently stay our progress.
— B. Washington

Artist: Judith Weller

Dedicated: 1984

Medium and size: Bronze (6.5 feet, seated), on granite pedestal (1 foot).

Location: Plaza in front of 555 Seventh Avenue, northwest corner of 39th Street. Faces west; best viewed in the early afternoon.

About the statue

In 1884, Meunier defied convention by sculpting the life-size, anonymous *Marteleur* at a time when over-life-size statues of famous men were the norm. A century later, anonymous figures had become common. Weller, turning the new norm around, made a statement about this nameless figure's importance by casting it in monumental size.

Like *The Immigrants* (cast about ten years earlier), *The Garment Worker* has a rough texture that blurs the distinction between hair, flesh, clothing and metal. Because this single figure is so much larger than life, however, the loss of detail is less detrimental than in *The Immigrants.*

Frowning slightly as he intently applies himself to the task at hand, *The Garment Worker* guides fabric into the sewing machine as his feet work the treadle. Is he hunched over with fatigue or with concentration? Impossible to say: perhaps both. What else? He's lean but not emaciated. He's Jewish—he wears a skullcap. He's poor, judging from his clothing. The bare table and the unpadded chair suggest a working day that's long and exhausting, with few distractions or moments of rest.

Booker T. Washington Bursting Up

If through me, a humble representative, seven millions of my people in the South might be permitted to send a message to Harvard that message would be, "Tell them that the sacrifice was not in vain. Tell them that by way of the shop, the field, the skilled hand, habits of thrift and economy, by way of industrial school and college, we are coming. We are crawling up, working up, yea, bursting up. Often through oppression, unjust discrimination, and prejudice, but through them we are coming up, and with proper habits, intelligence, and property, there is no power on earth that can permanently stay our progress."

—Booker T. Washington, speech at Harvard, 1896
(*A Treasury of Great American Speeches*, pp. 145-6)

About the subject

Many immigrants took whatever jobs they could manage with their limited knowledge of English and their few marketable skills. They were the labor force of New York's infrastructure: canals, railroads, aqueducts, sewers. They were also the backbone of the thriving ready-to-wear garment industry, which began to flourish after Elias Howe patented the sewing machine in 1846 and Singer improved it in the 1850s.

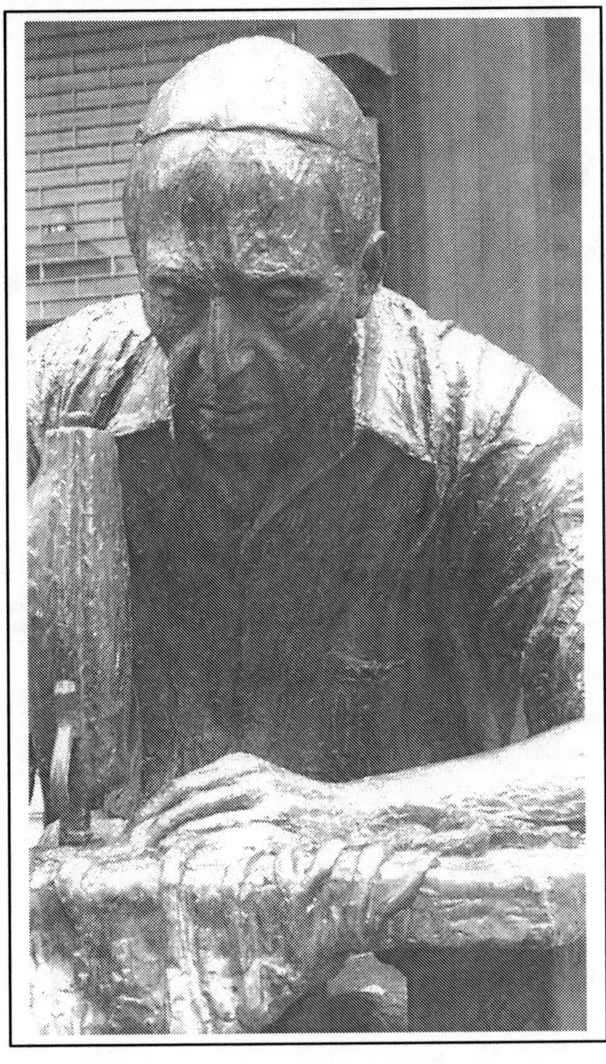

Art copyright © Judith Weller. Photo © Dianne L. Durante.

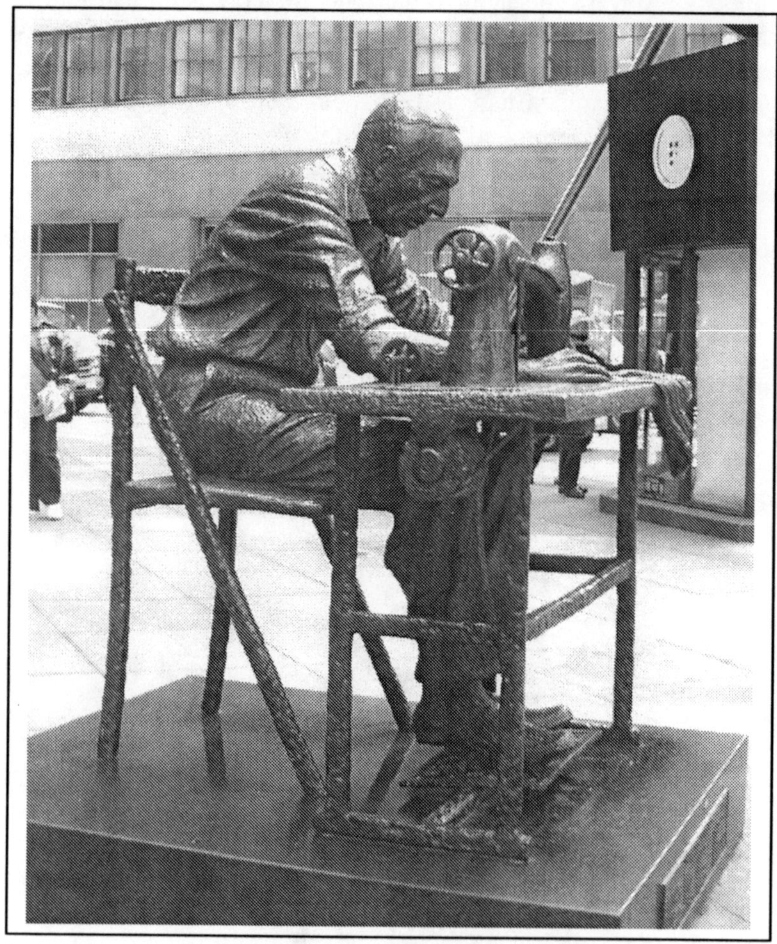

Art copyright © Judith Weller. Photo © Dianne L. Durante.

Such workers were not well paid, but most immigrants hadn't come to America expecting instant wealth. They were satisfied to have the freedom to earn it. (See Essay Number 14 on *The Immigrants.*)

This sculpture, which at first provokes pity, is an eloquent reminder of the ultimate success of many of those immigrants. Focus on the subject and you see a thin old man toiling at a tedious job. Focus on the fact that there's an over-life-size statue of such a man prominently displayed in New York's Garment District, and the perspective shifts. The more ambitious and energetic garment workers did not long remain in low-paying, tedious jobs. Like the former slaves described by Booker T. Washington (see sidebar), they improved themselves. By the 1880s, German Jews and their descendants owned 80 to 90 percent of the clothing firms in New York, the leading garment-manufacturing center in the United States. Today the descendants of workers such as this one can afford to erect monumental bronze statues honoring their ancestors.

Bibliography and further reading

Gayle & Cohen p. 149. SIRIS control #IAS 87870134.

On the rise of the garment industry in New York, see Burrows and Wallace, *Gotham* pp. 664-66 et al.; "Garment District" and "Garments" in *Encyclopedia of New York City*, pp. 451-53, both with bibliography.

Provenance

Sponsored by the International Ladies Garment Workers Union and the Public Art Fund. The plaque reads: "The Garment Worker by Judith Weller is donated to the City of New York by..." Should I include these forty-two names? Surely they deserve praise, even if in 10-point type, for helping fund a representational sculpture in the abstract 1980s. So here they are: "Affiliated Dress Mfg. Assn., Amalgamated Clothing & Textile Workers Union, American Cloak & Suit Mfg. Assn., Ann Klein, Apparel Dress Mfg., Assn. Of Rain Apparel Contractors, Bankers Trust Co., Bill Blass, Blouse Industry Trust Fund, Connecticut Dress Mfg. Assn., Anthony Conticelli, Crazy Horse, Ellen Tracy, Marty Gutmacher, Harve Benard, ILGWU, Isaac Hazen, Jeri Juniors, Jewish Communal Fund, Kat Kaplan, Stuart Kreigler, Ladies

Apparel Contractors Assn., Leslie Fay, Liz Claiborne, Maidenform, Main Line Fashions, Midtown Realty Owners Assn., Mori Lee, New Jersey Apparel, New York Coat and Suit Assn., Puritan Fashions, Ralph Lauren Womenswear, Rhapsody Blouse, Russ Togs, Abe Schrader, I. Safir, Sporteens, Sportswear Industry Trust Fund, United Better Dress Mfg. Assn., United Togs, Warner Communications, David Warren, 1984." Collection of the City of New York. On loan (according to the SIRIS database) to Swig, Weiler and Arnow, New York, NY.

Essay Number 16

1910

Samuel Rea

Back of the motor's humming, back of the belts that sing,
Back of the hammer's drumming, back of the cranes that swing,
There is the eye which scans them, watching through stress and
strain,
There is the mind which plans them—back of the brawn, the brain.

—Braley

Artist: Adolph A. Weinman

Dedicated: ca. 1910

Medium and size: Bronze, 10 feet high.

Location: Entrance to 2 Penn Plaza, Seventh Avenue at 32nd Street. Standing at the top of the Seventh-Avenue stairs to Penn Station, turn right and go up 6 steps. Bear left to the front of the building that rises over Penn Station. The statue faces east, and falls into shadow early in the day.

About the statue

Rea would not look out of place at a Wall-Street conference table today. From his well-groomed hair and mustache to his three-piece double-breasted suit, overcoat and hat, he is impeccably turned out. His upright posture, level gaze and unlined brow mark him as calm, confident and ready to deal with major projects or sudden crises. "Mr. Rea's appearance was that of a man of great strength and power," recalled the *New York Times* (3/29/1929). "He was more than six feet in height, and his strong, rugged face was surmounted by a shock of iron-gray hair. He would deal with tremendous problems and immense figures almost as with trifles, and while his associates often were struggling with a problem he would snap out his decision and the problem would be ended."

Rea carries a roll of plans for the Pennsylvania Station, and stands next to a model of part of the Station.

About the subject

"The station ... is the largest and handsomest in the world," declared the *New York Times* in 1910. "Any idea of it formed from description and pictures falls short of the impression it makes upon the eye." Commissioned in 1902, begun in 1906, completed in 1910, Pennsylvania Station was a magnificent building, from the steel and glass vaults of the concourse, to the coffered ceiling and arched windows of the waiting room, to the colossal columns and pediments of its exterior. (The General Post Office at Seventh Avenue and 34th Street, designed a decade later by the same architects, gives some idea of the monumental facade.) "No half-way solution should be attempted by the Pennsylvania Railroad Company," asserted Rea (1855-1929), who was in charge of the project to link the PRR's Jersey City terminal with Manhattan. "It should ultimately go into New York in such a manner as to answer the needs of the Company for the next half century at least, and on an equality with, if not on a more elaborate scale, than the New York Central and Hudson River Railroad Company."

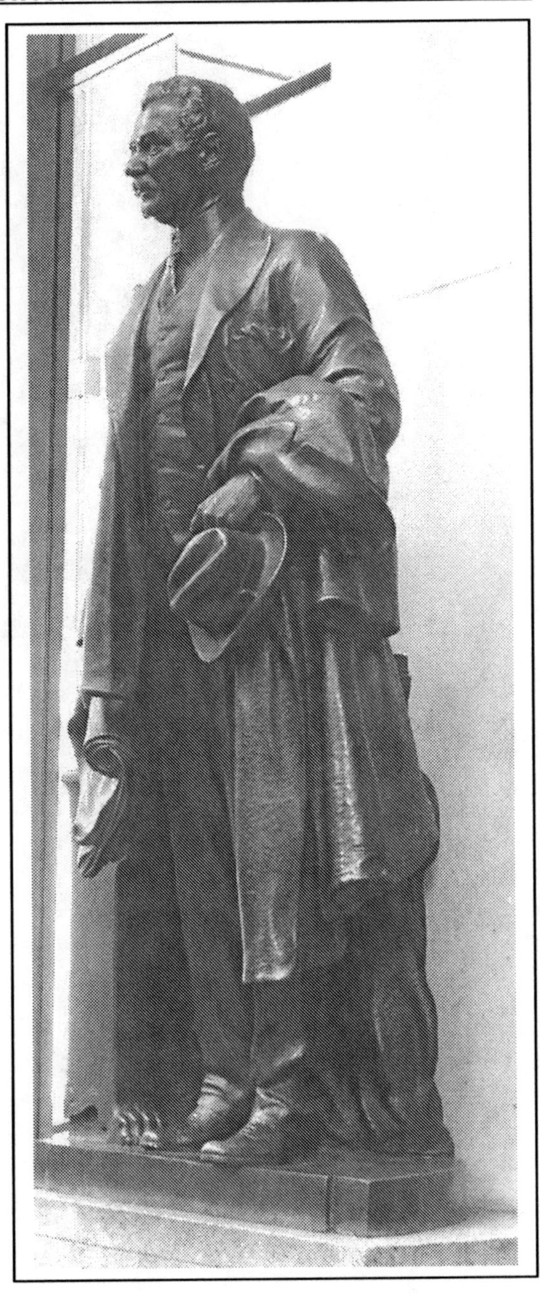

Photo © Dianne L. Durante

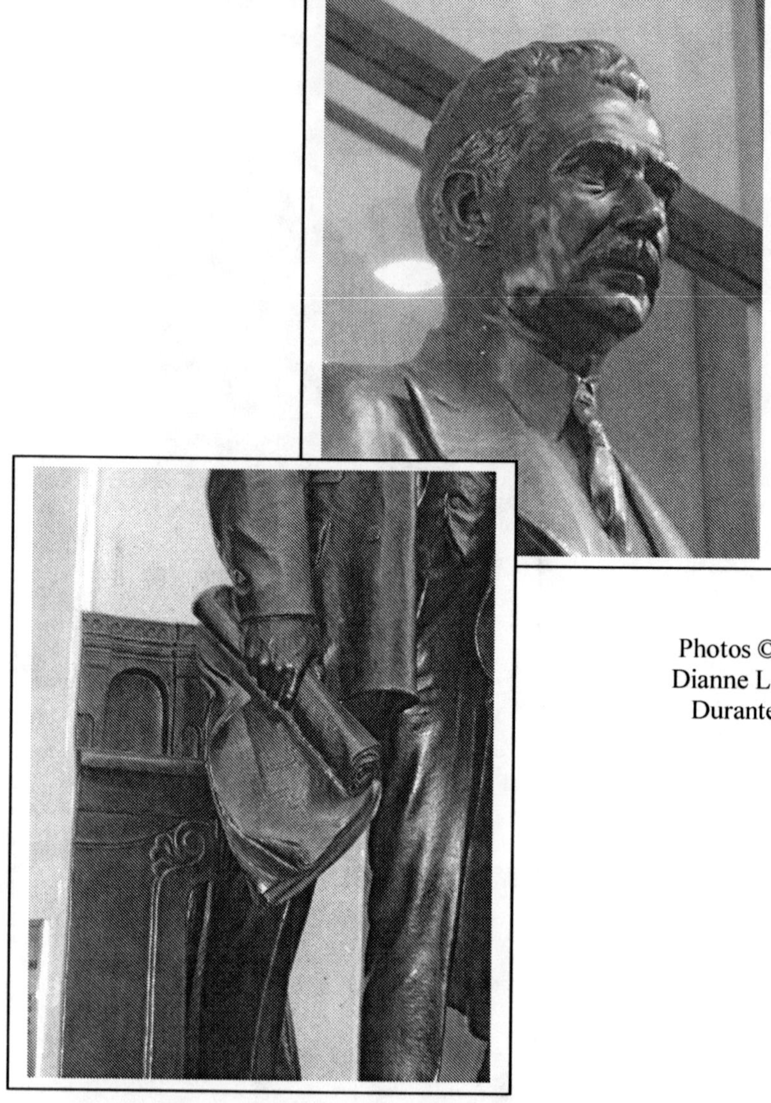

Photos © Dianne L. Durante

Like Cooper, Vanderbilt, Ericsson and Holley, Rea (who worked his way up from the lowliest ranks of the PRR) was the sort of man who knew how to persuade nature and his employees do his will:

> The drudge may fret and tinker, or labor with lusty blows,
> But back of him stands the Thinker, the clear-eyed man who knows. (See sidebar.)

The railroad tubes under the Hudson were the first such built in the Americas, designed by Rea after careful study of the recently constructed, electric-powered London subways. Another set of tubes sent trains under the East River to the sprawling railroad yards in Sunnyside, Queens, where cars were serviced, cleaned, and assembled into outgoing trains. This was one of the most massive engineering projects of the early twentieth century—matched only by the construction of Grand Central Terminal a few blocks away, by Vanderbilt's heirs.

A few years after the completion of the Pennsylvania Station, Rea was named president of the PRR, a position he filled with energy and dignity until 1925, when he reached the PRR's mandatory retirement age of seventy.

The tubes still carry trains under the Hudson and East Rivers. The Sunnyside Yards still service trains. But barely fifty years after its much-lauded completion, the Pennsylvania Station was torn down by the very company that built it. What happened?

Although Pennsylvania Station and Grand Central Terminal were under construction at the same time, the circumstances under which they were built were very different. The city and state of New York decreed in the 1830s that only two railroads, the New York and Harlem River Railroad and the Hudson River Railroad, would be allowed to run lines into Manhattan. Under Cornelius Vanderbilt's leadership, these and other railroads were eventually consolidated into the New York Central Railroad.

While Manhattan's business district was still centered on Canal Street, Vanderbilt bought relatively inexpensive land for a terminal at 42nd Street. In 1871 he finished the construction of Grand Central Depot on that site. Within twenty years, the New York Central's volume of traffic required an even larger building, completed in 1913: the present Grand Central Terminal.

The Pennsylvania Railroad was the New York Central's most efficient and aggressive competitor. Its operations extended from the East coast to the Mississippi River and from the Great Lakes to the Potomac. But for over forty years, PRR trains reaching New Jersey had to transfer passengers and freight to ferries in order to cross the Hudson River, because the PRR did not have legislative permission to build a railroad into Manhattan.

"The Thinker"

Back of the beating hammer by which the steel is wrought,
Back of the workshop's clamor, the seeker may find the thought.
The thought that is ever master of iron and steam and steel,
That rises above disaster and tramples it under heel.
The drudge may fret and tinker, or labor with lusty blows,
But back of him stands the Thinker, the clear-eyed man who knows.

For into each plow or sabre, each piece and part and whole,
Must go the brains of labor, which gives the work a soul.
Back of the motor's humming, back of the belts that sing,
Back of the hammer's drumming, back of the cranes that swing,
There is the eye which scans them, watching through stress and strain,
There is the mind which plans them—back of the brawn, the brain.

Might of the roaring boiler, force of the engine's thrust,
Strength of the sweating toiler—greatly in these we trust.
But back of them stands the schemer, the thinker who drives things through,
Back of the job, the dreamer, who's making the dream come true.

—Berton Braley, 1948

By the late 1800s, when the PRR was finally granted permission to run such a line, the commercial center of the city had shifted north to the mid-40s. The price of land forced the PRR to settle for a site on the west side of Midtown, where real estate was less in demand.

The Vanderbilts laid a multitude of tracks underground north of Forty-Second Street and sold the "air rights" over them for construction of hotels and apartment buildings. There was no such demand for space over the PRR tracks. Result: in contrast to the New York Central, the PRR was paying taxes on a property in Manhattan that was devoted solely to railroad traffic, with no offsetting income. (In 1970, after the PRR had merged with the Central and gone spectacularly out of business in the largest corporate bankruptcy in U.S. history, the biggest asset remaining to the company was not its trains, tracks or buildings, but the air rights north of Grand Central Terminal.)

Meanwhile, by the early twentieth century, railroads were increasingly hampered by government interference. In 1906, while Pennsylvania Station was under construction, the Interstate Commerce Commission was given the right to set "just and reasonable" rates for railroad freight and passengers. These rates could not be appealed in court. New labor laws favored unionization and higher wages. From 1900 to 1915 prices in the United States increased 35%. Wages of railroad workers increased 50%. Taxes paid by railroads increased 200%. During the same period the ICC permitted one rate increase for the railroads, of 5%. (See Schlichting p. 196.)

Furthermore, railroads were beginning to face serious competition for passengers and freight. By 1908 the first automobiles were being mass-produced in America. Over the next hundred years roads were built at public expense nationwide, including the Interstate Highway System (begun in 1956), and cars began to siphon off much of the PRR's lucrative passenger traffic. The government also funded the Port Authority Bus Terminal (less than ten blocks from Penn Station) and LaGuardia and Idlewild (now John F. Kennedy International) Airports.

By the 1950s, the PRR's major competitors—automobiles, buses, airplanes—had use of publicly financed and operated roads and terminals. Railroad travel during that decade fell to less than 25% of its peak during World War II. By the late 1950s, the PRR was running a $72 million deficit.

The multi-million dollar upkeep and operating expenses of Penn Station came out of the pocket of the PRR, which also paid over a million dollars a year in New York real-estate taxes. With no relief in sight for its steeply declining revenues, the PRR decided to reduce present and future losses by going into partnership with Madison Square Garden to build a smaller railroad station beneath a sports arena and office space.

The elegant home of the Chattanooga Choo-Choo ("You leave the Pennsylvania Station 'bout a quarter to four, / Read a magazine and then you're in Baltimore") was demolished in the early 1960s amid cries of horror that insensitive capitalists were destroying a historic building of tremendous architectural beauty and importance. But who destroyed Penn Station: the PRR, which paid for its demolition as well as its construction, or the local, state and federal officials who hampered and harassed the PRR until it could no longer afford to maintain Penn Station?

Bibliography and further reading

Gayle & Cohen p. 116. SIRIS control #IAS 87870109.

On Rea, see Robert L. Emerson, "Rea, Samuel" (http://www.anb.org/articles/10/10-01372.html, American National Biography Online Feb. 2000, with bibliography). On the original Penn Station, see William D. Middleton, *Manhattan Gateway, New York's Pennsylvania Station* (Kalmbach Books, 1996), and Peter Moore, photographer, *The Destruction of Penn Station*, edited and with an introduction by Barbara Moore (D.A.P. / Distributed Art Publishers, 2000). On Rea and the Pennsylvania Railroad in the early twentieth century, see *New York Times* articles of the period, especially those of 12/31/1901, 8/28/1916, 2/6/1922, 1/18/1924, 3/25/1929 and 3/26/1929.

On the construction of Grand Central Terminal, see Kurt C. Schlichting, *Grand Central Terminal: Railroads, Engineering, and Architecture in New York City* (Baltimore London, 2001), and *Transportation* in the forthcoming Forgotten Delights volume on allegories.

Provenance

Rea's statue originally stood in a niche within Penn Station. It now stands above and behind the Seventh Avenue entrance to the underground Station. The plaque, added after the statue was moved, reads: "Samuel Rea, Vice Pres. 1899-1912, President 1913-1925, Pennsylvania Railroad Company, under whose able supervision the Pennsylvania Station and the extension of the railroad serving it into New York City, was designed and constructed. The original station was opened to the public in September 1910 and was redeveloped, providing for Madison Square Garden Center above street level, during the years 1963-1968." Not owned by the City of New York; possibly owned by Amtrak or the Pennsylvania Station (see SIRIS).

Essay Number 17

1982

Double Check

That to secure these rights, Governments
are instituted among men ...
—*Declaration of Independence*

Artist: J. Seward Johnson, Jr.

Dedicated: 1982

Medium and size: Bronze (life-size), on metal bench (20 x 2.5 feet).

Location: temporarily in storage. Formerly at 1 Liberty Plaza, on Liberty Street between Broadway and Church Street.

About the statue

Intent on getting the details of the task at hand absolutely right, this well-groomed, well-dressed businessman is oblivious to passing crowds. Leaning over his open briefcase, he "double-checks" a memo on the letterhead of Merrill Lynch, the company that commissioned the statue. He could be Samuel Rea's colleague, or yours. Only a couple of the items in the briefcase—the clunky calculator and tape recorder—make him seem slightly outdated.

Both Johnson and George Segal are known for their sculptures of ordinary people, but the contrast between their styles is stunning. Segal's *Commuters,* in Port Authority Bus Terminal, is a line of three ghostly white figures with uniformly lumpy, rough surfaces. Segal's technique was to wrap models in fast-setting plaster bandages, then cast the cut-off bandages in bronze and apply a dull white patina (color fused to the bronze) to the whole. His technique preserved the most incidental details, from hairstyle to posture to overcoat buttons. (Segal once told the *New York Times* that the "unusual emotional reality" of his figures was due to the fatigue of his models: "To hold a pose for forty minutes, you can't be in a social or artificial posture." (6/10/2000). In addition, the figures' eyes are always closed, making them seem withdrawn from the world.

Johnson's sculptures, like Segal's, are ordinary figures shown life-size rather than monumental, but there the similarity ends. Johnson begins by sculpting a twelve-inch figure of his own design. Assistants enlarge it to a life-size nude to which clothes are attached, and Johnson then sculpts the head and hands. Thus it is Johnson, not a bone-tired, plaster-encased model, who determines the figure's proportions and height. Johnson can position the figure precisely as he pleases and rework details until he is satisfied, without concern for the discomfort or possible suffocation of his models. Sculpting the heads and hands allows the artist to include facial expressions and subtle hand gestures: again, not something Segal's technique permitted.

Since he works with clay rather than plaster bandages, Johnson can also set off parts of his work with varied textures. The hair is carefully distinguished from the face, the clothes from the briefcase. Finally, Johnson adds patinas to certain parts of the sculpture to make the figures even more lifelike. Here, for example, the shirt and paper are white, the hair and skin two different shades of brown.

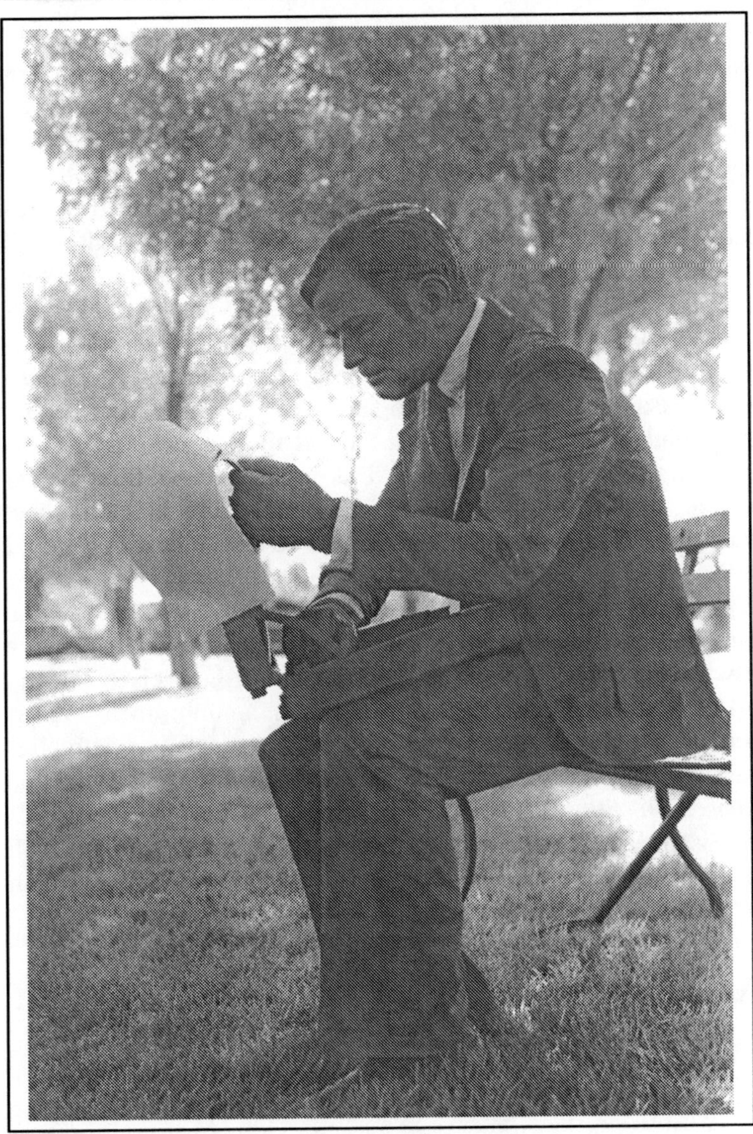

Photo courtesy of The Sculpture Foundation, info@TSFmail.com. Photo by Paula Stoeke. *Note:* The cast of *Double Check* described in this essay is presently in storage. This photo was not taken in New York.

As I said in the essay on *The Immigrants*, precise detail and extreme realism don't guarantee that an artist has anything worthwhile to say. Such details can, however, help the artist convey his message more passionately and forcefully, because they encourage the viewer to linger and study the work. If you doubt the importance of such stylistic details, imagine for a moment the figure in *Double Check* rendered in rough white with blindly staring eyes. Would you spend more or less time looking at it?

Art's purpose is not to reproduce what you can see by opening your eyes and looking about you. As noted in *The Immigrants* essay, art's purpose is to shout, "This is important! Stop, look, think about this!" At its best and most appealing, an artwork lets a viewer see the world as it can and ought to be (to paraphrase Aristotle)—or to see individuals such as Columbus, Ericsson or Rea, who drove themselves to do the best they could conceive.

Does anyone looking at Segal's *Commuters* ever think, with a warm glow of recognition: "That's me! That's how I am, that's how I want to be"? New Yorkers consider themselves not the sort of weary drudges Segal shows, but uncommon men, even if their uniqueness is recognized only by a few. The grateful figures in *The Immigrants* or the intent figure represented in *The Garment Worker* would not have aspired to become the bored, lifeless figures represented in *Commuters* – but they might well have aspired to be the figure in *Double Check,* a prosperous man performing a challenging task.

About the subject

How many of the items you've used so far today could you replicate—shaving cream, hair dryer, bagel, subway train, sneakers, CD player, eyeglasses? Next time you slide behind the wheel of your car, bite into a pizza, or commission a broker to invest your savings, take a minute to appreciate the division of labor that allows you to focus on what you do best, and to exchange your effort for the efforts of others who excel in very different fields.

Now consider what's necessary for such a division of labor, and all that's implied by the figure of a businessman on a park bench intently preparing for a meeting. A businessman could not long survive if his government didn't protect individual rights, including his right to profit from his ideas and to keep his earnings. Nor could he survive without the security and predictability provided by a government that enforced an objective code of law, defending him against foreign or domestic force and fraud.

No details of *Double Check* impel one to think about such political, economic, and ethical issues. To do so would require the sort of integration seen only in the greatest works of art. But if you are familiar with the principles required for a capitalist economy and a free society, you can certainly ponder them as you look at this bronze businessman.

September 11, 2001, was a brutal eruption of force and irrationality into New York's Financial District. *Double Check* was damaged by the fall of the Twin Towers, but unlike thousands of his human counterparts, he can be repaired. Before it is returned to Liberty Plaza, Johnson plans to rework the sculpture to incorporate a tribute to those who died at Ground Zero.

The Rights of Man and the Purpose of Government

We hold these truths to be self-evident, that all men are created equal, that they are endowed by their Creator with certain unalienable rights, that among these are Life, Liberty and the pursuit of Happiness. – That to secure these rights, Governments are instituted among Men, deriving their just powers from the consent of the governed...

– *Declaration of Independence*, 1776

Bibliography and further reading

Gayle & Cohen p. 28. SIRIS control #IAS 87870029. Special thanks to Paula A. Stoeke at The Sculpture Foundation for information on the ownership and status of *Double Check.*

On business and government, see Ayn Rand, *Capitalism: The Unknown Ideal*, especially "What Is Capitalism," "Man's Rights," and "The Nature of Government."

Provenance

Commissioned by Merrill Lynch; placed outside 1 Liberty Plaza when it was their headquarters. Owned by The Sculpture Foundation.

Essay Number 18

1983
Taxi

Productive work is the road of man's unlimited achievement and calls upon the highest attributes of his character ... — Rand

Artist: J. Seward Johnson, Jr.

Dedicated: 1983

Medium and size: Bronze (5.75 feet), no pedestal.

Location: Northwest corner of Park Avenue and East 47th Street. The statue faces south, and is easily visible until the shadows of the surrounding skyscrapers fall across it.

About the statue

A well-groomed, middle-aged but physically fit businessman steps briskly to the curb, one arm raised to hail a taxi, briefcase and raincoat tucked under the other. His mouth is open to shout, his brow wrinkled with intensity. As in *Double Check* at Liberty Plaza, Johnson has meticulously sculpted the details of the figure's face and hands, emphasizing variations in texture and adding patinas to the bronze to make it more realistic.

About the subject

An artist may claim to portray a "slice of life," but even when he shows what seems to be a random figure at a random moment, his choice of figure and moment inevitably reflect his own view of what's important. Perhaps Johnson decided to show someone hailing a cab simply because it's a common occurrence on Park Avenue. Nevertheless, it's significant that he shows a businessman rather than a socialite in an evening gown, a kindly grandfather, or a mother juggling a toddler and a stroller. It's equally important that Johnson chose to show a businessman who's mature, lean and energetic, so that he appears to be hailing a cab because he has an urgent appointment, not because he's too lazy or out of shape to walk.

Ayn Rand on Productivity

The virtue of Productiveness is the recognition of the fact that productive work is the process by which man's mind sustains his life, the process that sets man free of the necessity to adjust himself to his background, as all animals do, and gives him the power to adjust his background to himself. Productive work is the road of man's unlimited achievement and calls upon the highest attributes of his character: his creative ability, his ambitiousness, his self-assertiveness, his refusal to bear uncontested disasters, his dedication to the goal of reshaping the earth in the image of his values.

—Ayn Rand, "The Objectivist Ethics,"
The Virtue of Selfishness, 1964

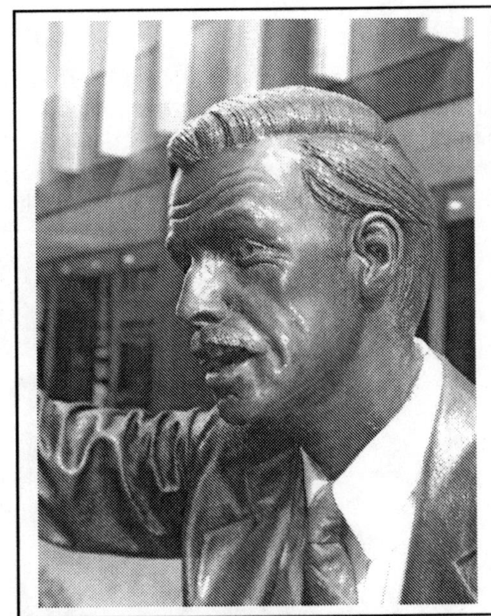

Image used by permission of The Sculpture Foundation, info@TSFmail.com. Photo © Dianne L. Durante

In its own quiet, unheroic way this statue, with its purposeful movement and energetic presence, reminds us to stop, look and think—to remember what's important and what we can aspire to. Although the famous men represented in the sculptures of *Forgotten Delights: The Producers* are long gone, their equals are with us today, creating and promoting everything from microchips and Internet access to convection ovens and sugar-free sweeteners. To the extent that you and I use our minds to support and improve ourselves—to the extent that we find a way to do even a trivial job a bit better, a bit more efficiently—we, too, are producers.

Bibliography and further reading

Gayle & Cohen p. 124. SIRIS control #IAS 87870113.

On Johnson, see the bibliography for *Double Check*.

On the implications of selectivity in art, including art that shows a "slice of life" (naturalism), see Ayn Rand, *The Romantic Manifesto* (New York, 1975), especially Chapter 6, "What Is Romanticism?"

Provenance

Plaque set in sidewalk: “Taxi by J. Seward Johnson, Jr. Commissioned by the Chemical Bank 1983.” Originally on Park Avenue at 48th Street, in front of the Chemical Bank headquarters. After Chemical merged with Chase and Chase with J.P. Morgan, the statue was moved a block south, in front of the J.P. Morgan Chase headquarters.

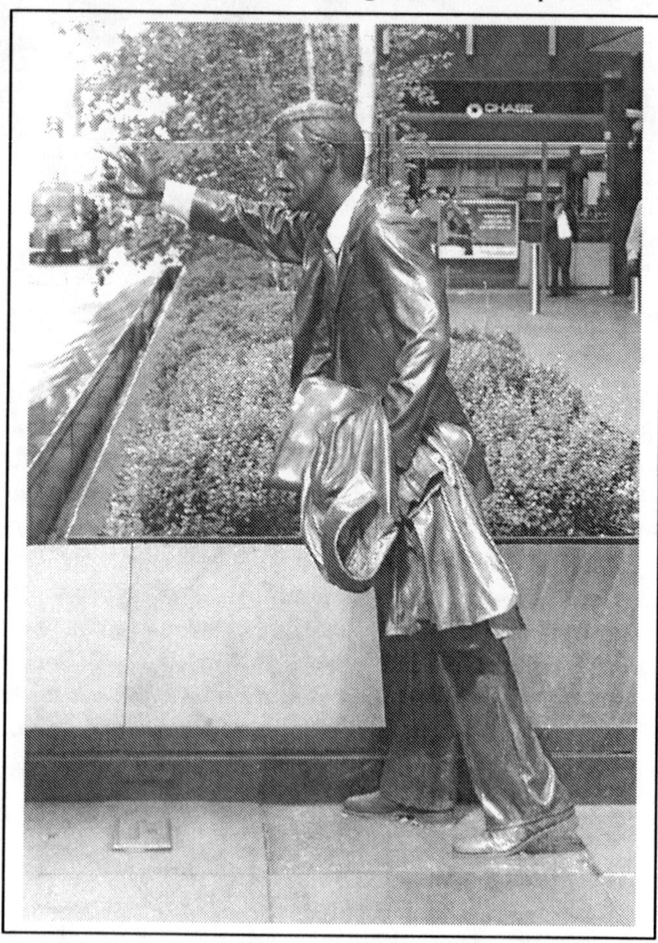

Image used by permission of The Sculpture Foundation, info@TSFmail.com. Photo © Dianne L. Durante

Essay Number 19

1988

Dreaming of Far Away Places:
The Ships Come to Washington Market

Here's honour to the builders—
The builders of the past;
Here's honour to the builders
That builded ships to last ...
—Lawson

Artist: Donna Dennis

Dedicated: 1988

Medium and size: Cut, welded, and painted steel fence, supported by brick piers. Each of the 14 sections is approximately 10 x 14 feet, and the fence runs about 224 feet along Greenwich and Chambers Streets. Thirteen hand-painted ceramic medallions, also by Dennis.

Location: Public School 234, at 300 Greenwich Avenue, on the southwest corner of Chambers Street. The fence, which runs along the north and east sides of the schoolyard, can be seen easily at any time. The medallions (on the east and south sides of the school building) are set at second-floor level, and rather difficult to see without binoculars.

About the statue

New York was founded and prospered as a port city and a commercial center. The steel fence of Public School 234 displays a flotilla of the type of ships that have brought people and products in and out of New York Harbor through the centuries: a square-rigged clipper ship, a tugboat, the Staten Island Ferry, a tanker, schooners, and a variety of small sailing ships. Near the site where the fence stands, the city in 1812 constructed a public market. By 1858 Washington Market was the largest food market in the United States, but (this will not surprise you if you've lived in New York City long) in 1859 it was closed down for causing traffic jams and for being the scene of rampant corruption. Rebuilt in the 1880s, the Market thrived for almost another hundred years. The retail section was shut down in 1956, and the wholesale section was replaced in 1967 by the enormous market at Hunts Point in the Bronx. The thirteen medallions along the school wall show Washington Market from its earliest times to the present.

About the subject

Looking at the ships on this fence—or at the real ones moored at nearby South Street Seaport or the Battery Park Marina—you might choose to focus on the fact that every one of them will someday sink, rot or be melted down for scrap. On the other hand, you might dwell on each ship's journeys to fabulous places, its cargoes of valuable goods, its excited passengers, and the decades it will be afloat. To focus on the positive doesn't mean you need willfully ignore the fact that someday each ship will cease to exist. It means you decide that the ship's end—

whatever it is, wherever it occurs—is not the single most important thing about it.

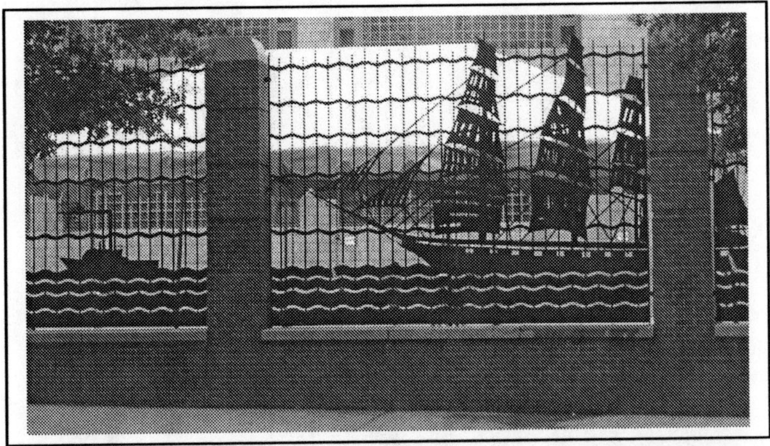

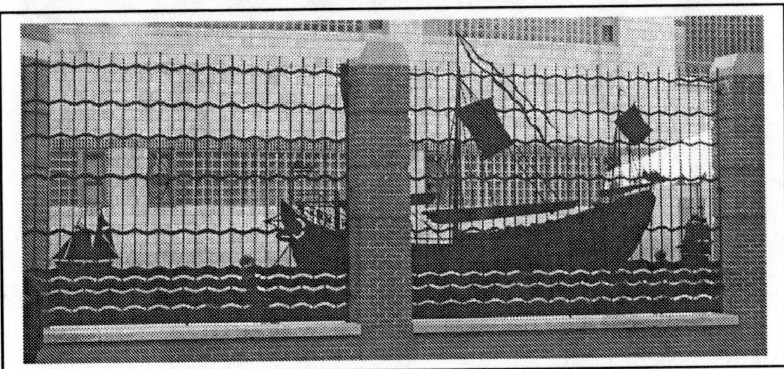

Art copyright © Donna Dennis. Photos © Dianne L. Durante

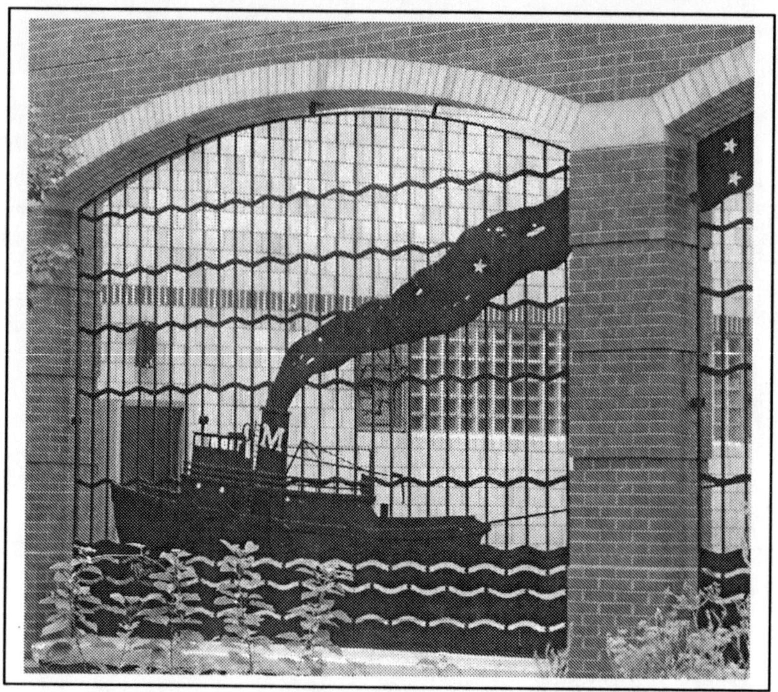

Art copyright © Donna Dennis. Photo © Dianne L. Durante

In *Forgotten Delights: The Producers* we have focused on the positive aspects of American business. That doesn't mean we need turn a blind eye to the wrongdoing and failure that can occur in the course of business. Choosing to focus on good businessmen is merely recognition of the fact that men who are productive and successful—"the men who won't go down" (see sidebar)—matter more than a relatively small number of failures and crooks.

In the Introduction I recounted my meetings with *John Ericsson.* When I finally found out what sort of man he was and why he had been honored, I didn't file him away under "problem solved." I discovered that I'd made a new friend, and that the sight of the old fuddy-duddy with mutton-chop whiskers, holding that strange oval object, now helps me remember my own values.

Looking at art can help you achieve such a focus on the positive, assuming you choose art that shows the world as it can and ought to be. Such art can also help you keep that focus—particularly if it stands in a public place where you pass it constantly.

All you need to do is stop, look, and think.

Bibliography and further reading

SIRIS control #IAS NY000051.

"The Ships That Won't Go Down" and many other poems by Henry Lawson (d. 1922) are online at http://members.ozemail.com.au/~natinfo/lawson/.

On art as emotional fuel, see Ayn Rand, "Art and Sense of Life," *The Romantic Manifesto.*

Provenance

Collection of the City of New York, Board of Education.

"The Ships That Won't Go Down"

We hear a great commotion
'Bout the ship that comes to grief,
That founders in mid-ocean,
Or is driven on a reef;
Because it's cheap and brittle
A score of sinners drown.
But we hear but mighty little
Of the ships that won't go down.

Here's honour to the builders -
The builders of the past;
Here's honour to the builders
That builded ships to last;
Here's honour to the captain,
And honour to the crew;
Here's double-column headlines
To the ships that battle through.

They make a great sensation
About famous men that fail,
That sink a world of chances
In the city morgue or gaol,
Who drink, or blow their brains out,
Because of "Fortune's frown."
But we hear far too little
Of the men who won't go down.

The world is full of trouble,
And the world is full of wrong,
But the heart of man is noble,
And the heart of man is strong!
They say the sea sings dirges,
But I would say to you
That the wild wave's song's a paean
For the men that battle through.

—Henry Lawson, d. 1922

Chronological List of Sculptures by Date Dedicated

1869 *Alexander von Humboldt,* by Gustaf Blaeser

1869 *Cornelius Vanderbilt,* by Ernst Plassman

1870 *Samuel Finley Breese Morse,* by Byron M. Pickett

1885 *The Pilgrim,* by John Quincy Adams Ward

1885 *William Earl Dodge,* by John Quincy Adams Ward

1890 *Alexander Lyman Holley,* by John Quincy Adams Ward

1892 *Columbus Monument,* by Gaetano Russo

1892 *Dr. James Marion Sims,* by Ferdinand von Miller II

1894 *Christopher Columbus,* by Jeronimo Suñol

1894 *Peter Cooper,* by Augustus Saint Gaudens

1903 *John Ericsson,* by Jonathan Scott Hartley (first version dedicated 1893)

1909 *Giovanni da Verrazzano,* by Ettore Ximenes

1910 *Samuel Rea,* by Adolph A. Weinman

1914 *Marteleur (Metalsmith),* by Constantin-Emile Meunier (sculpted 1884, first exhibited 1886)

1982 *Double Check,* by J. Seward Johnson, Jr.

1983 *Taxi,* by J. Seward Johnson, Jr.

1983 *The Immigrants,* by Luis Sanguino (designed 1973)

1984 *The Garment Worker,* by Judith Weller

1988 *Dreaming of Far Away Places: The Ships Come to Washington Market,* by Donna Dennis

Walking Tour of Sculptures in Forgotten Delights: The Producers

This tour can be done in one long day, or broken up into several expeditions. The sculptures are listed below from south to north in Manhattan. The number and letter in parentheses after the essay number refers to the statue's position in the grid on the maps on pp. 169-170. Don't forget the binoculars.

Essay #11 (1-D) *John Ericsson*
Battery Park, north end of Eisenhower Mall, between Castle Clinton and Battery Place.

Essay #3 (1-D) *Giovanni da Verrazzano*
Battery Park, near the waterfront, just east of Castle Clinton.

Essay #14 (1-D) *The Immigrants*
Battery Park, just north of Castle Clinton and southeast of *Ericsson.*

Essay #17 (2-D) *Double Check*
Originally at 1 Liberty Plaza, on Liberty Street between Broadway and Church Street. **Currently in storage.**

Essay #19 (3-C) *Dreaming of Far Away Places: The Ships Come to Washington Market*
Public School 234, at 300 Greenwich Avenue, just south of Chambers Street.

Essay #12 (5-C) *Alexander Lyman Holley*
Washington Square, west of the central fountain.

Essay #6 (5-D) *Peter Cooper*
Cooper Square south of the Cooper Union, where the Bowery splits into Third and Fourth Avenues.

Essay #16 (7-C) *Samuel Rea*
Entrance to 2 Penn Plaza, off Seventh Avenue at 32nd Street. Standing at the top of the Seventh-Avenue stairs to Penn Station,

walk right, go up 6 steps, then bear left to the front of the building over Penn Station.

Essay #15 (8-C) *The Garment Worker*

Plaza in front of 555 Seventh Avenue, northwest corner of 39th Street.

Essay #10 (8-C) *William Earl Dodge*

North side of Bryant Park, just south of 42nd Street and east of Sixth Avenue.

Essay #9 (9-D) *Cornelius Vanderbilt*

South facade of Grand Central Terminal, at the level of the Park Avenue viaduct. Pedestrians can enter the Hyatt Hotel (on 42nd Street just east of Grand Central), go up the stairs on the left to the reception level, go up the escalator to the left of Concierge's desk, then go through the revolving doors (ahead and to your right as you come off the escalator) to the sidewalk by the Park Avenue viaduct. Turn left on the sidewalk (toward 42nd Street), and follow the sidewalk around to the south side of Grand Central. The sidewalk ends almost across from the *Vanderbilt* statue.

Essay #18 (9-D) *Taxi*

Northwest corner of Park Avenue and East 47th Street.

Essay #1 (11-C) *Columbus Monument*

Columbus Circle, at the intersection of Eighth Avenue, Central Park South and 59th Street. The entrances to the island on which the monument sits are at the northwest and southwest sides of the Circle, by the new AOL Time Warner Center.

Essay #2 (11-C) *Columbus*

Central Park, south end of the Mall, near the Literary Walk. If the grid of the city streets ran through the Park, *Columbus* would be at about Sixth Avenue and 66th Street.

Essay #7 (11-C) *Samuel Finley Breese Morse*

Just inside Central Park at 72nd Street (near Fifth Avenue).

Essay #4 (12-C) *The Pilgrim*

Central Park, north of the 72nd-Street traverse. Walk into the Park at East 72nd Street, stay on the north side of the sidewalk, and you will see the statue up the hill to the right just as the 72nd-Street traverse splits into east- and west-bound lanes.

Essay #5 (12-C) *Alexander von Humboldt*
Central Park West at 77th Street, just east of the Museum of Natural History.

Essay #8 (14-C) *Dr. James Marion Sims*
Central Park at Fifth Avenue and 103rd Street, across from the Academy of Medicine.

Essay #13 (15-B) *Marteleur (Metalsmith)*
Columbia University, at the entrance to the Engineering Building (northeast corner of the campus, near Amsterdam Avenue and 120th Street).

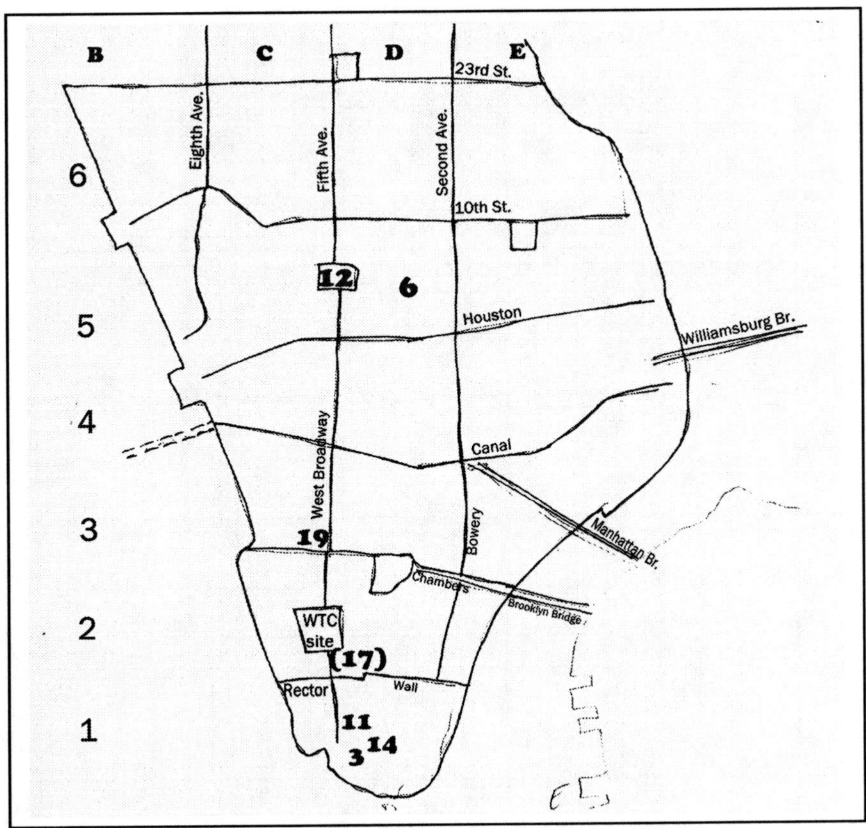

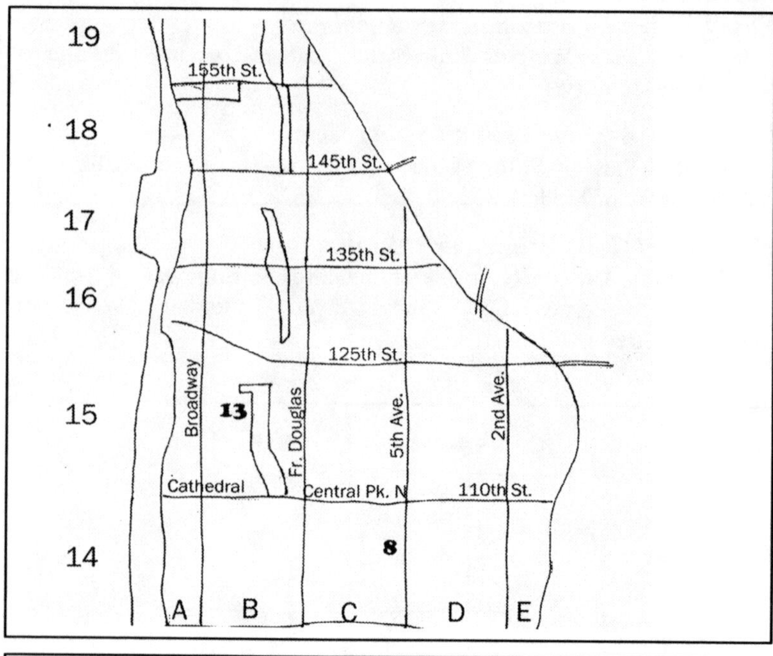
19
155th St.
18
145th St.
17
135th St.
16
125th St.
Broadway
13
Fr. Douglas
5th Ave.
2nd Ave.
15
Cathedral
Central Pk. N
110th St.
8
14
A
B
C
D
E

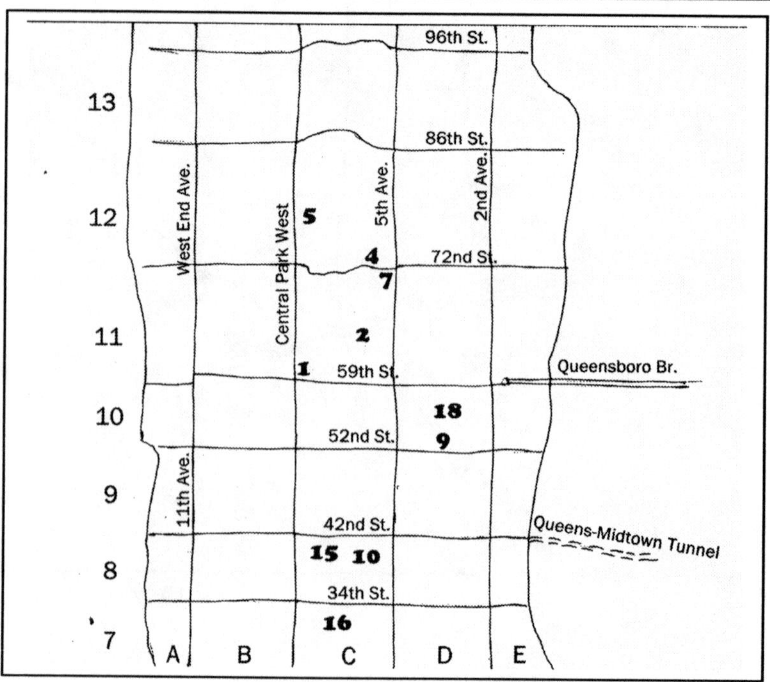
96th St.
13
86th St.
West End Ave.
Central Park West
5
5th Ave.
2nd Ave.
12
4
72nd St.
7
11
2
1
59th St.
Queensboro Br.
10
18
52nd St.
9
11th Ave.
9
42nd St.
Queens-Midtown Tunnel
8
15
10
34th St.
16
7
A
B
C
D
E

General Bibliography

References that apply only to specific sculptures are listed in the Bibliography section of each essay.

Books

American National Biography. Ed. John A. Garraty and Mark C. Carnes. Oxford University Press. Available online at major libraries.

Bogart, Michele H. *Public Sculpture and the Civic Ideal in New York City,1890-1930.* University of Chicago Press, 1989. Particularly useful for the City Beautiful movement of the late nineteenth and early twentieth centuries.

Burrows, Edwin G., and Mike Wallace. *Gotham: A History of New York City to 1898.* Oxford University Press, 1999. Remarkably detailed, Pulitzer-Prize winning history of New York, with a pronounced socialist slant; much useful information buried under mounds of statistics.

Gayle, Margot, and Michele Cohen. *The Art Commission and the Municipal Art Society Guide to Manhattan's Outdoor Sculpture.* Prentice Hall, 1988. Although Amazon reports the book out of print, it was available as of mid-2003 through the Art Commission's website (www.nyc.gov/html/artcom/html/publications.html).

Greene, Liza M. *New York for New Yorkers: A Historical Treasury and Guide to the Buildings and Monuments of Manhattan.* Second edition. W.W. Norton, 2001. Tracks the history of architecture in New York City from its foundation in the early seventeenth century to the present, through a chronological survey of New York's important monuments, buildings and sculptures. Over 600 small color photos with two or three sentences about each item. No index by location, so it can't be used as a walking guide.

Jackson, Kenneth T., ed. *The Encyclopedia of New York City.* Yale University Press and the New-York Historical Society,

1995. Extremely useful, copiously illustrated reference to all things New York, from "A&P" through "lawn bowling" and "John Lennon" to "Louis Zukofsky."

Reynolds, Martin. *Monuments and Masterpieces: Histories and Views of Public Sculpture in New York City.* New York, 1988. Focuses on the history of American sculpture by illustration of select pieces in New York City.

Stokes, Isaac Newton Phelps. *The Iconography of Manhattan Island, 1498-1909.* New York, 1915-1928; reprinted by the Arno Press, 1967. 6 vols. Volumes 4-5 are a massive compendium of events in New York for the past millennium or so, with references to newspapers and periodicals for the later entries.

Turner, Jane, ed. *The Dictionary of Art* (= *Grove Dictionary of Art).* London, 1996. 34 vols. The standard reference on artists and art history.

Websites

New York City Department of Parks and Recreation: http://www.nycgovparks.org/index.php. Includes the text of the green plaques placed near many city-owned sculptures.

Smithsonian Institution Research Information System (SIRIS): http://siris.si.edu. The Smithsonian American Art Museum's searchable inventory of painting and sculpture in the United States. Gives location, dimension, material, size, bibliography, and a few comments.

Subject Index

Notes

Notes

Printed in the United States
63676LVS00002B/28

9 780974 589916